PLAY BRIDGE WITH THE ACES

Learn to play your own top bridge game by playing top games along with The Aces.

In PLAY BRIDGE WITH THE ACES, Ira Corn Jr., the Dallas bridge expert and financier who set out in 1967 to create a world-champion bridge team made up of American players, shows how The Aces do it.

Whatever your level as a bridge player, there is only one way to play to your top capacity in the bridge game of the 1970s. You must know the method that is leading the competition now — the stimulating, exciting, self-perfecting, winning Aces method.

Play Bridge
with the Aces

Ira Corn Jr.

CORONET BOOKS
Hodder Fawcett Ltd., London

Printed and bound in Great Britain for
Coronet Books,
Hodder Fawcett Ltd,
St. Paul's House, Warwick Lane,
London, EC4P 4AH
by Hazell Watson & Viney Ltd,
Aylesbury, Bucks

ISBN 0 340 17314 9

CONTENTS

CHAPTER 1

INTRODUCTION

This book consists of bridge hands reported in The Aces' syndicated newspaper columns since June 1, 1970. Bridge hands can be entertaining and interesting to read, however, in addition, bridge columns offer an opportunity to the reader to learn to play better bridge. Should learning to play better bridge be one of your motives in reading this book, I want to explain briefly how you can best accomplish this objective.

Bridge is a fifty-two-card game. This simple statement is overlooked by many bridge players. All too often the bridge player thinks of the game as a thirteen-card game—the hand he holds—and then later if he plays the hand he thinks of it as a twenty-six card game; namely, his hand plus his partner's hand, which is the dummy. Actually, this is only part of the problem. By expanding your thinking of bridge to a fifty-two-card game you may now realize the importance of thinking about all fifty-two cards rather than just your hand and the dummy.

Bridge columns invariably report on fifty-two cards. To learn from bridge hands in the most effective manner, you must lay out the cards while reading the hand. This means that you should separate a deck of cards into the four hands shown.

Both play and defense of the hand are based on collection of information from four sources: (1) the bidding as it takes place; (2) the bidding that did not take place; (3) the opening lead and evaluation of the dummy; (4) the play of the cards as they unfold, one by one, including the lowest as well as the higher spots.

To facilitate bidding, bridge players have developed a number of systems and conventions for the purpose of making descriptive bids. These are called the "language of bidding." This language is limited to fifteen words. These consist of the numerals from 1 to 7, the four suits, and the words no-trump (to denote no suit), pass, double, and redouble. The objective is for you and your partner to develop a language which properly describes your card holdings to each other.

Your opponents have the same objective. Often they will use different bids, both artificial and natural, and it is necessary and legal that you know what each one of their bids means, just as it is necessary and legal that they know what each one of the bids you and your partner utilize means.

In order to properly interpret the opening lead and the play of the hand as it unfolds card by card, it is necessary to estimate and constantly revise that estimation as each card is played as to what cards you, your partner, and the opponents hold. Your hand provides thirteen of these cards, leaving thirty-nine cards distributed in the other three hands. Your hand, plus the dummy, provides twenty-six cards, leaving only twenty-six cards unknown. The bidding provides clues as to the likely holdings in the unknown hands. In addition to the information revealed in bidding and from the dummy, once it is exposed, the bridge player must have a working knowledge of card combinations and the likely way these cards may be played.

By studying the bridge hands in this book, and simultaneously laying the cards out on the table so that you can actually make the plays called for, you develop a meaningful interpretation of the cards that does not come across by merely reading the hand. Very few players, even bridge experts, can follow the bidding and play of the cards without actually laying the cards out for closer study so that interpretations can be made along the way which in turn leads to the best play.

The term best play generally refers to the best statistical probability of the likely distribution of the cards in view of the bidding, the play revealed to the point where a decision has to be made, and to an intuitive table presence which tends to provide interpretation of the intangible and qualitative happenings at the table involving the opponents which often provide clues as to the best way to proceed.

American people love to watch things as they actually happen. Surprisingly enough, people also love to watch things after they have happened. This is particularly true of athletics, such as football, tennis, and baseball. Often these same sports are shown on television hours and days after they actually took place and are still fascinating to the viewer. The same is true in bridge; however, bridge has an added advantage. By reading bridge hands one not only views what took place at the table but has the further advantage of being able to learn something about bridge so that they may put this knowledge into effect the next time they play the game. This fact adds an exciting dimension to such bridge books. You not only have the pleasure of viewing what took place when the hands were played, but also the option of learning something from the hands that can be valuable to you the next time you play bridge.

A brief résumé of bridge, the many different ways it is played, some of the strategy, and a thumbnail review of the bridge fundamentals are provided in Chapter 2. In the balance of this chapter, however, I would like to provide the reader with the current summary of bridge as a game widely played in the United States and as a competitive sport appealing to millions of people.

Over the past two decades a silent explosion has occurred in the world of American participant sports. Bridge has logged a tremendous growth of popularity, and it has done so silently, without enormous publicity or fanfare, without franchises— even without a national organization actively supporting the sport among non-players.

It is a sport that is a study in contrasts. It is horribly expensive or practically free; psychologically rewarding or totally ego devastating; played socially for fun or professionally for blood (and sometimes for blood at the social level); its players come in all sizes, all ages and all levels of ability; and there is even debate as to whether or not it is a sport.

Yet the fact remains, more than thirty million people play bridge, at some level, in North America. And that number will increase rapidly in the next decade if the experts are correct. About twenty-seven million of this number play rubber bridge alone, while some two and one-half million play social duplicate bridge. The remaining five hundred thousand have played over the past two decades in fiercely competitive and highly organized tournaments.

The boom in popularity of bridge which began in the early 1950s shows no signs of a slowdown. United States bridge teams won the World Championship for five years beginning in 1950; then for a fifteen-year period the famed Italian Blue Team dominated international bridge competition. In 1970, The Aces captured the world championship and successfully defended the title in 1971. Recapturing the World Crown for the United States has spurred interest in bridge to even higher levels.

No doubt bridge may well be the phenomenon sport of the '70s. In 1970, attendance at tournaments increased tenfold while the number of tournaments increased threefold when compared to twenty years ago. Some 750 tournaments were held in 495 cities on the North American continent last year;

1971 is up about 10 percent over 1970 in terms of both the number of tournaments and attendance.

Why has bridge become so popular in the last few years? First of all, it is an intellectual sport. You don't have to be big and husky or slender and fast to play. It is a great diversion for leisure time. It has become perhaps the most popular pastime for retired people. They have the spare time, they find the game intellectually stimulating, and it is very suitable for limited budgets. For social play, it is the least expensive of all competitive endeavors. An inexpensive card table, a pack of cards, a piece of paper and a pencil, and you're in business. If the budget is really tight, you don't even have to have the card table.

Tournament bridge is another kettle of fish entirely, however. Bridge is like golf, or bowling, or tennis in this respect. When a person goes to a tournament, he must spend several days at a hotel or resort. Hotel bills, food, and travel all add up rapidly. For the tournament bridge player, it is an expensive hobby.

Because it is a purely intellectual game, it can lift its players to heights of great satisfaction or completely shatter their egos. A good play can salvage an entire day. When a player or a pair do an exceptional job with a match, a hand, or even a single play, it is tremendously rewarding. When you goof, you are crushed. It's a shattering experience.

When you are beaten in a tennis match, for example, by a 16-year-old girl, you can rationalize the defeat. After all, she has youth and agility going for her. When you lose a bridge match, it simply means you've been beaten mentally. It's hard to take.

In the tournament world, women bridge players outnumber men by almost three to one. Men don't like to lose. They are conditioned from childhood to succeed—beat the other guy. But when you play bridge, you will lose more than you will win. Women can take a loss better than men, so they stay with the game.

Is bridge, in fact, a sport? Yes, it is a sport as brutal and as tough as professional football when it is played on the highest level. In championship bridge play, the hours are grueling, the concentration is tremendous, and it takes as much out of you physically as any sport.

Even social bridge has to be considered a sport. You are trying to win, trying to prove you are smarter than your opponent. You have to be mentally tough and you must stay alert. If that's not a sport, I can't define one. Well over five hundred books on bridge have been published in English since the Second World War.

With the growth in popularity, could bridge someday become a spectator sport as well as a participant sport? Yes! The Aces have staged eight full-scale exhibition matches, using Vu-Graph diagrams, commentators, and more recently, closed-circuit television techniques, as a test of the feasibility of bridge as a spectator sport. An exhibition using the best techniques to date was held in February 1971 in New Orleans. It drew an average of 940 paying spectators at each of four matches (capacity was some 1100) and can be classed as the most successful spectator bridge event ever held.

Moreover, on April 25, 1971, a one-hour special television show was televised coast to coast on the CBS network. It featured a very close match between The Aces and the Goren Stars, which The Aces won.

The Aces have compiled a remarkable record. During the past two years, out of the twelve major bridge events, The Aces have won eight; placed second, twice, tied for third, once; and seventh, once. This is the greatest record ever compiled by any American team over a two-year period.

CHAPTER 2

BRIDGE IN A NUTSHELL

Bridge is played in a surprising variety of methods. The strategies and tactics differ rather sharply. The three general approaches are as follows: (1) rubber bridge, also called social bridge or total points bridge; (2) match point duplicate; (3) IMP, or international match point, competition.

RUBBER BRIDGE TOTAL POINTS

This is the most widely played version of contract bridge. The term total points means that hands are scored according to traditional scoring methods on a cumulative basis. Growing in popularity is a second version of rubber bridge, called Chicago. The chief difference between Chicago and the customary scoring and play of rubber bridge is that in Chicago, an automatic rotation on vulnerability versus nonvulnerability is used for each four hands. On the first hand dealt, the dealer partnership is vulnerable; on the second hand dealt, the dealer is vulnerable and the opponents are not; on the third hand dealt, the dealer is vulnerable, the opponents are not; on the fourth hand dealt, both partnerships are vulnerable. This rotation continues throughout as further hands are dealt. In addition, in Chicago the scoring is on a single hand basis instead of total points accumulated. Each hand stands on its own so far as bonuses and depending upon results. An extract of the scoring schedule and basic rules on Chicago as set forth by The American Contract Bridge League is included at the end of this chapter. (Table One)

A new form of rubber bridge tournament competition was introduced by The Aces for the 1971 Hallmark National Rubber Bridge Championship. Approximately five thousand players competed in twelve geographical regions for the National title. The Finals were held in Las Vegas, a part of The Aces Hilton Bridge Festival held at the Las Vegas Hilton in December of 1971, with $45,000 total prize money for the two special matches.

The changes we devised included the following: (1) players carried forward their score; (2) except when bidding and making a slam or when opponents save against your slam, no pair could score more than 1100 points on a hand; (3) 500-point bonus for winning a set of four hands by more than 100 points; (4) split the 500-point bonus if the difference in scores is 100 points or less; (5) 300-point bonus if score is a blitz; (6) single hand scoring—Chicago style—4 hands to a round, 6 or 7 rounds of 4 hands each constitute a session; (7) Corn scoring, which permits establishing the winner within less than ten minutes after the session is complete.

MATCH-POINT DUPLICATE

This method of playing bridge permits comparison of results between a large number of competing pairs. The hands are dealt and remain intact in a special carrier (boards) and move in sequence along a number of tables so that all pairs sitting in the same direction will have played the identical hands. The pairs sitting in the opposite direction will have also played identical hands (the opposing twenty-six cards). For convenience, one direction is referred to as North-South and the other East-West. Each direction is considered a field of its own and the results achieved by each pair holding the identical twenty-six cards are compared and converted to a match point score.

The match point score on each deal is determined as follows. A pair is awarded 1 match point for each pair whose result is less than theirs and a half match point for each result tied.

The following chart is an example involving a deal played between five different sets of contestants. (There is no limit on the number of times the hand can be played. However, the time factor usually places the optimum upper limit at fourteen tables.)

The results on Board #1 varied. Three North-South pairs (#1, 2, and 3) bid and made four spades and earned 2 match points, an average score. (4 match points was maximum; therefore, half of that is average.) These pairs earned the 2 match points for bettering the result of pair #5 (1 point) and for tying the results of two other pairs (two half points).

Pair #4 scored 10 more total points than those who made four spades and had the best result of all competing pairs. They therefore earned the maximum number, or 4 match points (a "top").

Pair #5 scored less than any other pair and earned no match points (a zero).

13

Board No. _____ 1

N-S Pair#	E-W Pair#	Contract	By	Made	Down	Final Score N-S	Final Score E-W	Match Pts. N-S
1	1	4 S	S	4		420		2
2	3	4 S	S	4		420		2
3	5	4 S	S	4		420		2
4	7	3 NT	N	4		430		4
5	9	4 S	S		1		50	0

14

At the end of the session, usually twenty-six hands, the match points won by each pair on each hand are added together and the winning pair is the pair having the highest total.

Match-point duplicate is the most widely played form of tournament bridge. The strategy in this game is significantly different from bridge played according to total points. The reason is because an absolute limit exists on how many points you can lose on any one hand. You may go down four, doubled and redoubled, but you can get no less than a zero, and the effect of that zero is no more than zero out of a possible maximum total of twelve (or whatever number is top). If twelve is top, the winning duplicate score on the average would be the score of a player who could average between 7 and 8 points per hand, so that a pair playing duplicate could score zero on one hand and two 12s on the next two hands, and thereby end up with an average of 8 points per hand, which would be enough to assure a shot at winning overall if that average could be maintained. The winning match-point duplicate player is the player who can best calculate the probabilities of a given bid or play at the table which would put him in the upper range of scoring 7 to 12 points on a comparative basis with the other players who will also hold that specific hand. His tactics might vary sharply at the table in order to achieve the extra overtrick, which might, in and by itself, endanger the contract, but if successful would effect a good score. The impact on your total score is precisely the same if you bid one no-trump and make an extra overtrick when no one else is able to do so, as when you bid seven no-trump and make seven when all other pairs were in and making seven spades. In both instances, you would score an absolute top. Much of the emphasis in match point duplicate, therefore, deals with part-score strategy as well as game and slam strategy. In addition, match point duplicate strategy varies, depending upon the tactics employed when playing seeded pairs as compared to the tactics employed against nonseeded pairs.

A section of a tournament event usually consists of fourteen tables. Three or four of the fourteen pairs are seeded in order to assure proper distribution of the higher ranking pairs throughout the entire tournament. In playing twenty-six hands against the thirteen other pairs ordinarily found in one session of duplicate, the winning player has to employ different tactics against the seeded players compared to the tactics employed against the nonseeded pairs.

IMP TEAM PLAY

The highest caliber of bridge competition combined with bridge competence is found in team bridge. This form of bridge utilizes a unique combination of (1) single-hand scoring and (1) IMP (international match point) scoring. It is the finest form of rubber bridge and may also be scored total points without seriously affecting the excitement of the game. Single-hand scoring is applied to the results on each hand at one table. The same hand is replayed with different team members sitting different directions and the results are then compared with the initial results obtained by the opposing team on the same hand. Both the single-hand scoring and IMP scale are given at the end of this chapter. (Table Two) For example, on a specific hand at one table, the opposing team playing the same hand bid four spades and made five, for a score of plus 450. The score at the other table is 420 (making four only). The difference is 20 points, and this equals 1 IMP. This difference is inconsequential in team bridge and total points, but in match-point bridge, even this small margin might be the difference between a top and an average. To continue, in team bridge, if one team scored 420 at one table and, on the same cards, the opposing team scored 420 (four spades bid and made), then there would be no gain or loss. This would be, in effect, a tie, or in bridge jargon, a push. On the other hand, if one pair of The Aces bid and made four spades at one table and at the other table another pair of The Aces, defending against the same cards, were able to defeat the opponents by one trick in their four-spade contract, then this would constitute a major swing in favor of The Aces. The Aces would be plus in both rooms, 420 for bidding and making four spades in one room, and 50 for having defeated the same four-spade contract in the other room, for a total gain of 470 points. By looking at the IMP table, you can see that the 470 converts to 10 IMPs, a significant gain.

IMP bridge is the form of competition utilized in determining the World's Champion each year, and in determining the winner of the two most prestigious national bridge competitive events in the United States—the Vanderbilt in the spring of each year, and the Spingold in the summer. IMP bridge has a great deal more similarity to total-points bridge than match point duplicate. In fact, during the first two years of training of The Aces, one of the significant rules laid down was that The Aces were to avoid playing match-point events. It tends to negatively affect the ability to compete with the highest degree of skill in IMP bridge.

16

The bridge hands reported in this book refer to the kind of competition involved, because this often affects the bidding and play of the hand in terms of tactics and strategy. These variations help distinguish between the different kinds of contract bridge widely played in the United States.

ACES' POINT COUNT

Charles Goren, in his basic bridge textbook published in 1942, popularized point-count bidding. The Aces' count is an improved method of point counting with a strong shift in emphasis, though the fundamentals remain the same. The two significant evaluation principles developed in bridge during the past twenty-five years which have been demonstrated to be notably more important than was originally thought to be the case when the Goren point-count approach first became popular are: (1) Aces are worth more proportionately than the ratio of four, three, two, one allows, and this value is greater if your hand has more than one ace, even greater if your hand has more than two aces, and so on. Aces' point count gives credit for 1 extra point for each ace in excess of one held in the hand to be evaluated. For example, if you have two aces, then the point count from the aces held would be nine. If your hand holds three aces, the point count would be fourteen. (2) Distributional values have far greater playing strength than given credit for in the original Goren point-count approach. For example, a hand with six spades, five hearts, a singleton diamond and a singleton club is so strong that it should be opened with as little as nine or ten points. (A-J-10 9-7-2, K-J-4-3-2, void, and 6-2). This has become nearly standard practice today. The best way to show this kind of distribution is to get into the bidding early. This gives your partner an opportunity to visualize his hand as compared to yours.

The original Goren point count is given at the end of this chapter. (Table Three) The Aces' count is summarized as follows:

THE DIFFERENCE BETWEEN NO TRUMP AND SUIT BIDDING; THE "ACES COUNT"
(Extracted from "Aces Standard" by Ira G. Corn, Jr.)

Even a bridge novice, after his first session at the table knows that there is an enormous difference between play in no-trump and play with a trump suit. In suit play you can win tricks when the opponents lead a suit in which you are void. In no-trump, when you are void in a suit you cannot take tricks when that suit is led. Long, strong suits will take tricks in both no-trump and suit contracts, but they are more certain to win tricks in no-trump, where the opponents cannot trump. On the other hand, if your long suits are not solid, they can be established more easily in suit play, where you can trump your losers.

These differences, which become quite obvious after just a few dozen hands of bridge, have led me to the conclusion that there should be two different methods for evaluating the strength of a hand; one to be used if the final contract is in no-trump, the other for suit contracts. I use the point count in each case to count the high card points, but there are three major differences:

1. Do not count distributional points if the likely contract is in no-trump.

2. If the final contract is going to be in a suit in which the partnership has a "fit," add one point if you hold two aces, and add two points if you hold three or four aces.

3. If the final contract is going to be in a suit, jacks count one point only if they are accompanied by the ace, king, queen or 10. Otherwise they count zero.

I call this the "Aces Count" (with all due apologies to those who dislike puns), and it seems to me that it gives a much more accurate evaluation than other methods. Its basic features can be summarized by its name; aces count more than any other card in suit play, and they are actually worth more in suit contracts than they are in no-trump.

I think that this approach to bidding is substantially superior to all other methods of evaluating points. Since it is so different from other methods, I have not only called the method by a new name (the "Aces Count"), but I will use one terminology in this book in dealing with suit bidding, and another in dealing with no-trump auctions. Here is the distinction: (1) in no-trump bidding, we count high card points (HCP); (2) in suit bidding, we count Aces Count points (ACP).

Thus, in what follows, I will be talking in terms of two entirely different kinds of points. In no-trump auctions, we are going to be concerned with HCP, the simple value of your honor cards. In suit auctions, however, we are going to be counting ACP, which more accurately measure the power of trump fit and controls. Aces really do count for more in suit play than in no-trump, and that greater power is more readily apparent in the use of ACP than by mechanically adding up high cards. Further, while unsupported jacks may well serve as secondary stoppers in no-trump contracts, they are often

18

useless in suit contracts unless they are combined with other honors in the same suit. Thus, an unsupported jack counts for zero ACP, even though it gets 1 HCP for no-trump bidding. So, for example, this hand:

♠ A 6 4 3
♥ A 8 5
♦ A 7 5 2
♣ 6 3

is worth only 12 HCP in a no-trump contract, but it is worth 15 ACP in a suit contract (you add 2 points for holding three aces, and 1 point for the doubleton), unless the trump suit is Clubs.

Before we get into the actual procedures of opening the bidding and responding, I want to take a moment to analyze the real theoretical basis for the Aces Count, for it will help you throughout your bridge-playing career. Why is an ace worth more than 4 points in a suit contract? Let's take a look at a simple hand:

♠ A K J 10 9 8
♥ 3
♦ A K Q J 10 9
♣ Void

♠ Q 7 6 5 4 3
♥ K Q J 10
♦ Void
♣ K Q 10

I have taken this extreme case to show the tremendous power of aces in suit contracts. In this hand, if South held the ace of hearts instead of the K-Q-J-10, he could make seven spades. Obviously, the ace would be worth more than the K-Q-J-10, yet the K-Q-J-10 counts for 6 points, and the ace is worth only 4. Why this difference in evaluation? The answer is simple: the standard point count (HCPs) is geared to no-trump, and *in no-trump the K-Q J-10 can be quickly developed into three tricks, while the ace will only take one trick.*

Examples:

	POINT COUNT		
	STANDARD	ACES	
♠ A K 10 3 2	7	7	
♥ A 4 2	4	4	
♦ K 9 2	3	3	
♣ 6 5	1	1	
	15	15	
		1	2 Aces
		16	

♠ K J 7 2	4	4	
♥ Q 10 9	2	2	
♦ K Q 7	5	5	
♣ A Q 6	6	6	
	17	17	
		0	1 Ace
		17	

♠ A Q J 10 2	7	7	
♥ A 10 9 8 4	4	4	
♦ 10 2	1	1	
♣ 6	2	2	
	14	14	
		1	2 Aces
		15	

♠ A J 10 9 6 2	5	5	
♥ A 10 8 4 2	4	4	
♦ 3	2	2	
♣ 2	2	2	
	13	13	
		1	2 Aces
		14	

NATURAL SYSTEMS

Bridge systems follow two wide patterns. First, and the most popular American practice, is to bid using natural methods. This term means that you bid your hand in such a way as to tell your partner what you have, so your partner can better evaluate his hand, and vice versa. The Goren system, Kaplan/Sheinwold, Roth-Stone, and nearly all standard American systems are based on natural methods. There is still some difference of opinion between opening four-card majors as against five-card majors, but in any event, the systems are natural. Depending on the partnership understanding, the bids of natural systems reflect generally what each partner holds. Various specialized conventions are employed by the bidders using natural methods to further describe specific holdings through a variety of devices. Aces Scientific, played by Aces Bobby Goldman and Mike Lawrence, employs basically natural methods with a wide variety of conventions and special bidding techniques. This system is a superb illustration of a natural bidding system combined with intricate, specialized devices to indicate special strength and distributional holdings.

Most American systems are aimed at success in match points in tournament play rather than IMP play. A large number of players, particularly in social rubber bridge, continue to play Culbertson, the earliest form of a natural bidding approach.

ARTIFICIAL SYSTEMS

Most U.S. players prefer a system in which it is possible for them to arrange for a wide variety of partners on short notice. This generally cannot be accomplished if you play artificial systems, thus the strong preference for a natural system. It is not likely that a random partner has devoted enough time to learn thoroughly an artificial system, and therefore, if you require new and infrequent partners to play an artificial system, it can lead to many misunderstandings. The chief advantage of playing Goren, Culbertson, or Kaplan/Sheinwold is that a wide number of other players are already familiar with these systems. Therefore, artificial systems, while well-known in the United States, are not widely used. Some of the better known artificial systems include the Vanderbilt Club, the Schenken Club, the Neapolitan Club, the Roman Club, the Precision Club, and the Big Diamond. These systems are based on two fundamental premises: (1) that one hand which has certain perimeters of strength may make a series of forcing bids which elicit from partner a response about the shape and strength of the partner's hand, and that this will help arrive at the best contract; (2) the emphasis in this exchange of information is placed upon the possession of "controls" (aces and kings) so that at low levels the forcing bidder has full knowledge of the partnership's possession of aces and kings, as well

21

as (on certain occasions) specific suit holdings. The theory is that both of these facts, once obtained, enable the forcing bidder to better determine the final contract. Artificial systems are of real value if you have well-established partnerships. They have found their greatest success in playing team bridge. In recent years, the Precision Club system, developed by C. C. Wei, has gained increasing popularity in the match-point duplicate tournament world. This method of bidding has proved more adaptable to match-point bidding than the other artificial systems.

Table One
FOUR-DEAL BRIDGE
CHICAGO*

Four-deal bridge is a form of rubber bridge much played in clubs and well suited to home play. Its effect is to avoid long rubbers of uncertain duration; a member never need wait longer than the time (about twenty minutes) required to complete four deals. The game is also called club bridge, and is often known as Chicago for the city in which it originated.

A. *BASIC RULES:* The Laws of Contract Bridge and Rules for Club Procedure are followed, except as modified by the following rules.

B. *THE RUBBER:* A rubber consists of a series of four deals that have been bid and played. If a deal is passed out, the same player deals again and the deal passed out does not count as one of the four deals.

A fifth deal is void if attention is drawn to it at any time before there has been a new cut for partners or the game has terminated; if the error is not discovered in time for correction, the score stands as recorded. A sixth or subsequent deal is unconditionally void and no score for such a deal is ever permissible.

In case fewer than four deals are played, the score shall stand for the incomplete series unless attention is drawn to the error before there has been a new cut for partners or the game has terminated.

When the players are pivoting,† the fact that the players

---

*(Reprinted by permission of American Contract Bridge League)
†In a pivot game, partnerships for each rubber follow a fixed rotation.

have taken their proper seats for the next rubber shall be considered a cut for partners.

C. *VULNERABILITY:* Vulnerability is not determined by previous scores but by the following schedule:
First deal: Neither side vulnerable.
Second and Third deals: Dealer's side vulnerable, the other side not vulnerable.
Fourth deal: Both sides vulnerable.

D. *PREMIUMS:* For making or completing a game (100 or more trick points) a side receives a premium of 300 points if on that deal it is not vulnerable. There is no additional premium for winning two or more games, each game premium being scored separately.

E. *THE SCORE:* As a reminder of vulnerability in four-deal bridge, two intersecting diagonal lines should be drawn near the top of the score pad, as follows: The numeral 1 should be inserted in the angle thus formed that faces the first dealer. After play of the first deal is completed, 2 is inserted in the next angle in clockwise rotation, facing the dealer of the second deal. The numerals 3 and 4 are subsequently inserted at the start of the third and fourth deals respectively, each in the angle facing the current dealer.

A correctly numbered diagram is conclusive as to vulnerability. There is no redress for a bid influenced by the scorer's failure to draw the diagram or for an error or omission in inserting a numeral or numerals in the diagram. Such error or omission should, upon discovery, be immediately corrected and the deal or deals should be scored or rescored as though the diagram and the number or numbers thereon had been properly inserted.

F. *PART SCORES:* A part score or scores made previously may be combined with a part score made in the current deal to complete a game of 100 or more trick points. The game premium is determined by the vulnerability, on that deal, of the side that completes the game. When a side makes or completes a game, no previous part score of either side may thereafter be counted toward game.

A side that makes a part score in the fourth deal, if the part score is not sufficient to complete a game, receives a premium of 100 points. This premium is scored whether or not the same side or the other side has an uncompleted part score. There is no separate premium for making a part score in any other circumstances.

G. *DEAL OUT OF TURN:* When a player deals out of turn, and there is no right to a redeal, the player who should have dealt retains his right to call first, but such right is lost if it is not claimed before the actual dealer calls. If the actual dealer calls before attention is drawn to the deal out of turn, each player thereafter calls in rotation. Vulnerability and scoring values are determined by the position of the player who should have dealt, regardless of which player actually dealt or called first. Neither the rotation of the deal nor the scoring is affected by a deal out of turn. The next dealer is the player who would have dealt next if the deal had been in turn.

H. *OPTIONAL RULES AND CUSTOMS:* The following practices, not required, have proved acceptable in some clubs and games.

(1) Since the essence of the game is speed, if a deal is passed out, the pack that has been shuffled for the next deal should be used by the same dealer.

(2) The net score of a rubber should be translated into even hundreds (according to American custom) by crediting as 100 points any fraction thereof amounting to 50 or more points: *e.g.,* 750 points count as 800; 740 points count as 700 points.

(3) No two players may play a second consecutive rubber as partners at the same table. If two players draw each other again, the player who has drawn the highest card should play with the player who has drawn the third-highest, against the other two players.

(4) Any player may announce, prior to the auction and before he has looked at his hand, which deal it is and who is vulnerable; or may for his own information, inquire as to these facts when it is his turn to call. There is no redress if no announcement is made or if incorrect information is given.

(5) To avoid confusion as to how many deals have been played; each deal should be scored, even if there is no net advantage to either side, for example, when one side is entitled to 100 points for undertrick penalties and the other side is entitled to 100 points for honors. In a result that completes a game, premiums for overtricks, game, slam, or making a dou-

bled contract should be combined with the trick score to produce one total, which is entered below the line (for example, if a side makes two spades doubled and vulnerable with an overtrick, 870 should be scored below the line, not 120 below the line and 50, 500 and 200 above the line.)

Table Two
THE SCORE

DUPLICATE CONTRACT BRIDGE SCORING

The rubber bridge scoring table applies to duplicate bridge with the following exceptions: trick points scored on one board do not count toward making game on a board subsequently played; premium points are scored for making a part score or game, not for winning a rubber; honors are not scored in match-point or international match-point play.

DUPLICATE BRIDGE SCORING

TRICK SCORE

Scored by *declarer's side*, if the contract is fulfilled:

For each odd trick bid and made	IF TRUMPS ARE ♣	♦	♥	♠
Undoubled	20	20	30	30
Doubled	40	40	60	60
Redoubled	80	80	120	120

	AT A NO-TRUMP CONTRACT		
	Undoubled	Doubled	Redoubled
For the first odd trick bid and made	40	80	160
For each additional odd trick	30	60	120

A trick score of 100 points or more, made on one board, is GAME. A trick score of less than 100 points is a PART SCORE.

PREMIUM SCORE

Scored by *declarer's side*:

SLAMS

For making a SLAM	Not vulnerable	Vulnerable
Small Slam (twelve tricks) bid and made	500	750
Grand Slam (all thirteen tricks) bid and made	1000	1500

For each OVERTRICK	Not vulnerable	Vulnerable
(tricks made in excess of contract)		
Undoubled	Trick Value	Trick Value
Doubled	100	200
Redoubled	200	400

PREMIUMS FOR GAME, PART-SCORE, FULFILLING CONTRACT

For making GAME, vulnerable 500
For making GAME, not vulnerable 300
For making any PART SCORE 50
For making any doubled or redoubled contract 50

HONORS

Scored by either side at total-point play,
not at match-point play:
For holding four of the five trump HONORS
(A-K-Q-J-10) in one hand 100
For holding all five trump HONORS
(A-K-Q-J-10) in one hand 150
For holding all four ACES
in one hand at a no-trump contract 150

UNDERTRICK PENALTIES

Scored by declarer's *opponents* if the contract is *not* fulfilled:

UNDERTRICKS........

(tricks by which declarer fails to fulfill the contract)	NOT VULNERABLE			VULNERABLE		
	Un-doubled	Doubled	Re-doubled	Un-doubled	Doubled	Re-doubled
For first undertrick	50	100	200	100	200	400
For each additional undertrick	50	200	400	100	300	600

INTERNATIONAL MATCH POINT SCORE

The International Match-Point scale effective September 1, 1962, is as follows. The difference in the scores made at the two tables on each deal is converted into international match points on the basis of this scale.

Difference in Points	IMP	Difference in Points	IMP	Difference in Points	IMP
20— 40	1	370— 420	9	1500—1740	17
50— 80	2	430— 490	10	1750—1990	18
90—120	3	500— 590	11	2000—2240	19
130—160	4	600— 740	12	2250—2490	20
170—210	5	750— 890	13	2500—2990	21
220—260	6	900—1090	14	3000—3490	22
270—310	7	1100—1290	15	3500—3990	23
320—360	8	1300—1490	16	4000 & upwards	24

Table Three
STANDARD POINT COUNT

HONOR CARDS

Ace = 4   King = 3   Queen = 2   Jack = 1

The point count value of the honor cards (excluding 10s) totals 40 points for each deal.

Distributional point count values differ with each deal in accordance with the long suits and short suits dealt to each player.

Distributional point count is as follows:

Initial Evaluation

Doubleton	1 point
Singleton	2 points
Void	3 points

Support Evaluation

Doubleton	1 point
Singleton	3 points
Void	5 points

(when holding good support for a suit partner has bid.)

When any honor card other than an ace is held alone, it is subject to losing some of its value. Any aceless hand is also slightly overvalued. You should deduct one point when evaluating an aceless hand or when holding a singleton honor lower than an ace.

27

Key Numbers

Game in no-trump (count only high card points)	26 HCP
Game in spades or hearts	26 points
Game in diamonds or clubs	28+ points
Small slams	33 points
Grand Slams	37 points

EXAMPLES OF POINT COUNT

		HCP		Distribution
1.	♠ A J 8 7 2	5		
	♥ K J 5 4 3	4		
	♦ K 7	3		1
	♣ 9			2
		12	+	3
2.	♠ 10			2
	♥ A 8 5 3	4		
	♦ J 6 4 2	1		
	♣ K Q J 3	6		
		11	+	2
3.	♠ Q 7 6	2		
	♥ K Q 9	5		
	♦ A J 8 5 2	5		
	♣ Q 4	2		1
		14	+	1
4.	♠ A Q J 10 7	7		
	♥ A K J 10 2	8		
	♦ K	3	−1*	2
	♣ Q 4	2		1
		19	+	3
5.	♠ A K 6	7		
	♥ Q 7 5	2		
	♦ K Q J	6		
	♣ J 10 8 4	1		
		16	+	0

(4) Deduct one point for singleton honor.

28

		HCP	Distribution
6.	♠ K J 9 6	4	
	♥ K 10 8 2	3	
	♦ Q J 10	3	
	♣ Q 5	2	1
		12* +	1
7.	♠ J	1 −1*	2
	♥ K J 5 4	4	
	♦ A J 4 3	5	
	♣ K J 7 6	4	
		13	2

(6) Deduct one point for Aceless hand.
(7) Deduct one point for singleton honor.

A word about evaluation of unguarded honors. For purposes of simplicity we have recommended that one point be deducted for any singleton honor lower than an ace. There are various ways to evaluate doubleton queens, tripleton jacks, etc. The fact of the matter is that initial hand evaluation is but a guide to be changed in accordance with new information available to you as the bidding unfolds. The value of an unguarded honor increases if your partner holds good values in the same suit (which is quite probable if he bids the suit) and conversely, the value of an unguarded honor decreases if your opponents hold good values in the same suit (which is quite probable if the opponents bid the suit).

Stated as a general rule, "Promote unguarded honors to full value when partner bids the suit. Demote unguarded honors to little or no value if the opponents bid the suit."

CHAPTER 3

PLAYING BRIDGE WITH THE ACES

A BRIDGE PLAYER'S NIGHTMARE
"The Wolff in Wolf's Clothing"

A favorite diversion of bridge players is to dream up a
nightmare hand and then wish it upon their worst enemy.
Bobby Wolff of The Aces had just such a dream recently. He
sat his archenemy in the South seat while he was holding the
East hand, trying hard to suppress an evil grin.

North-South vulnerable
Dealer South

```
                        NORTH
                        ♠ 9 4 3
                        ♥ Q 7
                        ♦ Q 9 7 6
                        ♣ J 8 5 4

                                        (Wolff, the
                                        good guy)
        WEST                            EAST
        ♠ K                             ♠ J 2
        ♥ J 10 9                        ♥ K 8 5 4 3 2
        ♦ K 10 3                        ♦ J 8 5 4 2
        ♣ 10 9 7 6 3 2                  ♣ —
                        (The bad guy)
                        SOUTH
                        ♠ A Q 10 8 7 6 5
                        ♥ A 6
                        ♦ A
                        ♣ A K Q
```

The bidding:

South	West	North	East
2 ♠	Pass	2 NT	Pass
3 ♠	Pass	4 ♠	Pass
6 ♠	Pass	Pass	Pass

Opening lead: Jack of hearts.

In Wolff's dream he made North-South vulnerable so South would feel worse after he finished the hand. Furthermore, he gave him a hand that he could never forget.

The bidding was direct, and South quickly contracted for a small slam in spades.

Wolff, of course, knew what everyone had, so he did not double for a club lead. He knew that a club ruff would spoil his diabolical plans. After a club ruff, declarer would have no choice but to win any return and lay down the ace of spades and, when the remaining spades obligingly fell, declarer would then be able to discard his losing heart on the Jack of clubs.

Oh, no, Wolff was too smart for that. Instead, he had his partner lead the jack of hearts—this was his dream wasn't it? When the queen was played from dummy, Wolff played small! (If he covered, declarer, having no dummy entry, would be forced to make seven by plunking down the ace of spades.)

Declarer was overcome with this good fortune. West had apparently led away from the king of hearts, giving dummy an otherwise impossible entry. The entry to the dummy now made it possible for declarer to make a safety play in spades. Declarer was a good enough player to realize that the only way he could go down after the queen of hearts held the trick was if East had K-J-2 of spades and declarer failed to finesse.

So naturally declarer led a trump from dummy. Wolff played low—ever so cunningly low—and the declarer finessed the queen. West pounced upon this trick and returned a club, which Wolff trumped.

Now Wolff laughed and laughed—so hard that South came at him with murder in his heart. But it was too late. Wolff woke up before any harm could befall him. And, oh, how he enjoyed that dream!

Those of us who have played the game seriously for some time have encountered such nightmares. Bridge is a game that can cause many nightmares. The laws of chance sometimes seem to be purposely directed against us.

One of the secrets to winning bridge is to remain philosophical throughout your nightmare periods. Like the winning golfer who must play each shot individually, the winning bridge player does not allow an occasional nightmare to affect the other deals left to play.

CUE BIDDING
"You Clever Little Devil You!"

Cue bidding has become a fine art these days. More and more players want to know what it's all about so they can join the fun. They don't realize that cue bidding can be dangerous when the partner misconstrues it as a natural bid. One of the all-time spectacular misunderstandings took place a few years ago when this very thing happened.

North-South vulnerable
Dealer South

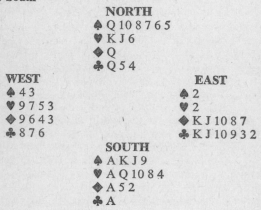

```
                    NORTH
                 ♠ Q 10 8 7 6 5
                 ♥ K J 6
                 ♦ Q
                 ♣ Q 5 4
   WEST                            EAST
 ♠ 4 3                           ♠ 2
 ♥ 9 7 5 3                       ♥ 2
 ♦ 9 6 4 3                       ♦ K J 10 8 7
 ♣ 8 7 6                         ♣ K J 10 9 3 2
                    SOUTH
                 ♠ A K J 9
                 ♥ A Q 10 8 4
                 ♦ A 5 2
                 ♣ A
```

The bidding:

| Guiver | | Lawrence | |
South	West	North	East
2 ♣	Pass	2 ♦	3 NT
4 NT	Pass	6 NT	Pass
7 C!	Pass	Pass! !	Pass

Opening Lead: Three of diamonds.

Bidding like this requires an explanation. South was Harold Guiver, Long Beach, Calif., bridge expert. North was Mike Lawrence, now a member of The Aces, but then (thank heavens) playing independently.

Guiver's two-club opener was an artificial forcing bid, with an intention to show his suit at the next opportunity. Guiver-Lawrence were using weak two bids, thus the two-club opening.

Lawrence responded with two diamonds to deny any strong suit. As it turns out, two spades would have worked much better. East now gummed up the works something awful by bidding three no-trump which he intended as an unusual no-trump overcall to show the minors.

Guiver, now somewhat flustered, bid four no-trump, a bid that to this day remains somewhat of a mystery. Lawrence, equally befuddled, thought it was some sort of a natural bid (he reasoned it couldn't be Blackwood as no suit had been agreed upon, let alone mentioned) and raised confidently to six no-trump.

Guiver now began to have second thoughts over this auction. He reasoned that, since East had made an unusual no-trump overcall for the minors, surely Lawrence would realize that a seven-club bid at this point would be a takeout for the majors!

Lawrence, strangely enough, failed to grasp the innate cunning of the bid, simply thought that Guiver had long clubs, and passed! Harold's face gave away nothing—perhaps someone would double and he could get out.

No such luck. Everyone passed and West led a small diamond. Lawrence, not realizing he had passed a cue bid, decided to be tricky as he put down the dummy. He reasoned that the queen of clubs was a fantastically good card to hold on this bidding and carefully put it down last, tabling two small trumps originally.

When he finally placed the queen of clubs down triumphantly on the table, Guiver, still showing no emotion, said, "Oh, you clever little devil, you."

MOMENT OF INDECISION
"Goldman Trades a Headache for an Upset Stomach"

How many times have you heard the cliché, "Aces were made to take kings"? Unlike many other bright sayings of bridge, a player who follows this advice will be right far more often than wrong. However, there is always the exception.

The exception is easily overlooked—even in a world championship. Observe the defense of today's hand played in a match between The Aces and China in the 1971 Bermuda Bowl championship. Ace Bobby Goldman (West) went wrong in today's hand. However, he was the first to admit it.

None vulnerable
Dealer North

                        NORTH
                        ♠ K J
                        ♥ K 10 8 4
                        ♦ K Q 9 4 2
                        ♣ A K

WEST   EAST
♠ Q 10 7 4 3   ♠ 8 6 5 2
♥ A Q 9 6   ♥ 7 2
♦ A J 10   ♦ 5 3
♣ 6   ♣ 8 5 4 3 2

                        SOUTH
                        ♠ A 9
                        ♥ J 5 3
                        ♦ 8 7 6
                        ♣ Q J 10 9 7

The bidding:

North	East	South	West
1 ♦	Pass	1 NT	2 ♦
Dbl.	2 ♠	3 ♣	Pass
3 NT	All pass		

Opening lead: Four of spades.

Over South's one no-trump response West, Goldman, cue-bid two diamonds, describing a hand with major suit length. Not wishing to defend against two spades, North-South pressed on to the three no-trump game.

Goldman (West) opened his fourth best spade and declarer played dummy's king in order to preserve the spade ace as an entry to his clubs. The ace and king of clubs were cleared from dummy to make way for declarer's clubs. Next came dummy's diamond king and Goldman's moment of decision. He took the king with his ace—a decision he would later regret.

Goldman cleared the spades (playing the queen) and declarer ran his clubs. On the play of the last club, the position was:

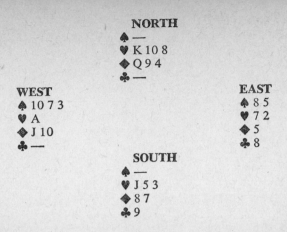

NORTH
♠ —
♥ K 10 8
♦ Q 9 4
♣ —

WEST
♠ 10 7 3
♥ A
♦ J 10
♣ —

EAST
♠ 8 5
♥ 7 2
♦ 5
♣ 8

SOUTH
♠ —
♥ J 5 3
♦ 8 7
♣ 9

Goldman had no safe discards. A red suit discard was obviously suicidal. Goldman discarded a spade and dummy a heart. Declarer then played hearts to make the contract. Goldman took only two spades, one heart and one diamond.

Observe the effect if Goldman had refused the diamond ace. Declarer would have been stranded in dummy and would have had to commit himself. Declarer could not lead another red card, since Goldman could win cheaply and clear the spades while he still held both aces. If declarer played a spade to run the clubs, then all Goldman had to do would be to hold his two aces and his three long spades.

The Aces won the match convincingly, scoring the maximum victory points possible. However, when I congratulated the players on their victory, Goldman was quick to point out his lapse on today's hand. A good reason why The Aces play as a team instead of a group of individuals.

TRICKY DEFENSE
"Dr. Charlie Chases the King"

The city of Fort Worth hosted The Aces in their first exhibition match since retaining their world championship title. The Fort Worth Star-Telegram and the Goodfellows sponsored the highly successful show seen by over four hundred spectators.

Although The Aces jumped off to an early lead, the remainder of the match was in Fort Worth's favor and the challengers reduced The Aces' winning margin to a final 38 international match points.

Witness the play of today's exciting hand by Dr. Charles Robinson of Fort Worth, which gave the partisan crowd much reason to cheer.

Vulnerable North-South
Dealer South

<pre>
                    NORTH
                    ♠ 8
                    ♥ K 10 4
                    ♦ Q J 9 2
                    ♣ A K 9 7 3
    WEST   EAST
    ♠ A J 10 4 2   ♠ K 9 5
    ♥ A 8 5 3   ♥ 9 7 6
    ♦ K   ♦ 6 5
    ♣ J 10 6   ♣ Q 8 5 4 2
                    SOUTH
                    ♠ Q 7 6 3
                    ♥ Q J 2
                    ♦ A 10 8 7 4 3
                    ♣ —
</pre>

The bidding:

South	West	North	East
Pass	1 ♠	Dbl.	Pass
2 ♠	Pass	3 ♣	Pass
3 ♦	Pass	4 ♦	Pass
5 ♦	All pass		

Opening lead: Ace of spades.

North made a take-out double of West's opening bid of one spade and Dr. Robinson (South) forced with a cue-bid of two spades. Over the expected three-club response, Dr. Robinson showed his diamonds and then continued to game after North's raise.

The results of the closed room showed that Aces Jim Jacoby and Bobby Wolff had played the same contract and had made it for 600 points to The Aces. Dr. Robinson had to equal this result to gain a tie and the viewing audience knew it was not going to be easy. Since two aces had to be lost, all depended on declarer capturing West's singleton trump king.

West opened with the spade ace and followed with the heart ace. Two tricks for the defense. At the third trick, West led another heart, won by declarer's jack.

Dr. Robinson now made a good play. He played his spade queen in an effort to get West to cover if he had the king of spades (the opening lead of the ace may have been a false card).

When West followed low to the queen of spades, Dr. Robinson ruffed in dummy and led the diamond queen. When East followed the 5, declarer played his ace, felled West's king and made his contract. The crowd applauded enthusiastically, since this result kept a strong Fort Worth rally alive.

Considering only the trump suit, the percentage play was a finesse. Why did Dr. Robinson play to drop the king?

After he assured himself that West had not led the spade ace from an original holding of A-K, he correctly deduced that West had to have the diamond king as part of his opening bid. If so, only a singleton king would yield the contract.

Excellent analysis and play of an exciting hand in an exciting match.

LOSING THE SETTING TRICK
or
"Partner, How Could You Be Such a Jerk?"

Whose ears have never rung with the question, "Partner, how could you not take the setting trick?"

Most of us learn to avoid this embarrassing question early in our bridge life. Inevitably, an exception to make us sorry for learning our lesson never fails to appear.

Today's hand was such a backfire. It was played in the 1970 world pairs championship in Stockholm.

None vulnerable
Dealer East

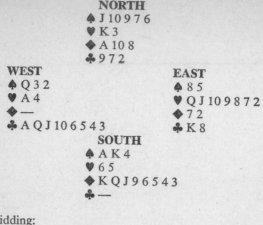

NORTH
♠ J 10 9 7 6
♥ K 3
♦ A 10 8
♣ 9 7 2

WEST
♠ Q 3 2
♥ A 4
♦ —
♣ A Q J 10 6 5 4 3

EAST
♠ 8 5
♥ Q J 10 9 8 7 2
♦ 7 2
♣ K 8

SOUTH
♠ A K 4
♥ 6 5
♦ K Q J 9 6 5 4 3
♣ —

The bidding:

East	South	West	North
3 ♥	5 ♦	6 ♣	6 ♦
Pass	Pass	Pass	

Opening lead: Ace of hearts.

As is often the case after preemptive bids, distributional values, coupled with lack of bidding space, serve to produce a lively auction. No one can be sure of his best course, and it is difficult to resist the temptation to bid once more. Today's auction was no exception.

West opened the ace of hearts, which held the trick. At trick two he had a problem. Should he try to cash his ace of clubs?

He was fairly certain that South had another heart and could not discard a possible club loser on the heart king. However, suppose South had a doubleton A-K of spades, which would enable him to establish the spade suit for club discards?

West could already hear the searing question, "Partner, how could you not take the setting trick?" He played the ace of clubs!

South ruffed the ace of clubs and played the diamond king and a low diamond to dummy's ace. Dummy's club 7 was now ruffed, East playing his king. South cashed the ace of spades and ran all his diamonds to produce this position:

38

NORTH
♠ J
♥ K
♦ —
♣ 9

<table>
<tr><td>WEST</td><td></td><td>EAST</td></tr>
<tr><td>♠ Q 3</td><td></td><td>Immaterial</td></tr>
<tr><td>♥ —</td><td></td><td></td></tr>
<tr><td>♦ —</td><td></td><td></td></tr>
<tr><td>♣ Q</td><td></td><td></td></tr>
</table>

SOUTH
♠ K 4
♥ 3
♦ —
♣ —

When South led the heart three to dummy's king, West could not discard safely. If West discarded a spade, South's K-4 of spades would take the last two tricks. If West discarded the club queen, dummy's 9 would become a winner.

West could have defeated the hand only by continuing a heart at trick two. This would remove the vital entry to dummy and save West from the trap.

Remember this hand the next time you might feel the impulse to ask, "Partner, how could you not take the setting trick?"

HINDSIGHT'S BETTER
"How Many 'Hearts' Have You Broken?"

The Aces and the Omar Sharif Bridge Circus played in St. Paul, Minn., at the famous Twin Cities winter carnival. After the exhibition one night, transportation back to the hotel was impossible. The match had been played in the auditorium, and the streets were jammed with festivities.

The players were far from cheerful as they braced themselves for the snow. "Rome or Dallas was never like this," they lamented.

"We should have made that slam," said Giorgio Belladonna to Billy Eisenberg. Both had gone down on the same hand.

In spite of Giorgio's reputation as one of the toughest members of the famed Italian Blue Team, some doubtful eyebrows were raised. Challenge and counter-challenge ensued, and the generation of heat was not unwelcome.

This was the hand which tripped Giorgio and Billy.

Both vulnerable
Dealer South

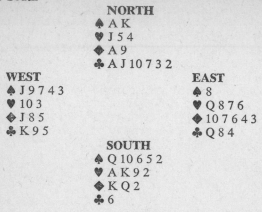

```
                    NORTH
                    ♠ A K
                    ♥ J 5 4
                    ◆ A 9
                    ♣ A J 10 7 3 2
   WEST                              EAST
   ♠ J 9 7 4 3                       ♠ 8
   ♥ 10 3                            ♥ Q 8 7 6
   ◆ J 8 5                           ◆ 10 7 6 4 3
   ♣ K 9 5                           ♣ Q 8 4
                    SOUTH
                    ♠ Q 10 6 5 2
                    ♥ A K 9 2
                    ◆ K Q 2
                    ♣ 6
```

The bidding:

Eisenberg		Goldman	
South	**West**	**North**	**East**
1 ♠	Pass	2 ♣	Pass
2 ♥	Pass	2 ♠	Pass
2 NT	Pass	3 ♣	Pass
3 NT	Pass	4 NT	Pass
5 ◆	Pass	5 ♥	Pass
5 ♠	Pass	6 ♠	Pass
Pass	Pass		

Opening lead, Three of hearts.

The bidding was not as complex as it appears. Once Gold-man bid two clubs, all bids below game were forcing and in-vestigatory. Four no-trump was natural and slam invitational. Five diamonds accepted and showed one ace. Five hearts asked South to select the suit.

The slam was a reasonable one and required only a little luck for success.

The opening lead gave Billy great hopes. He played low from dummy and East played the queen, which was won by Billy's king.

With the fall of the heart 10, Billy could claim the slam if he could hold his losses to one-trump trick. He played two high trumps in great anticipation, but East's discard smashed all hope.

Belladonna did not suffer as much as Billy. His hopes were not fired by the disappearance of a probable heart loser on opening lead. However, he also played trumps at the first opportunity and joined Billy in misery.

How can the hand be made? "Easy," said Belladonna, chastising himself in the process. This, he explained, is how he should have played:

Win the lead of the diamond 5 in dummy. Play ace of clubs and ruff a club. Play K-Q of diamonds, discarding a heart from dummy. A low spade to dummy's king and another club ruffed. Now A-K of hearts and a third heart West ruffs and dummy overruffs. This is now the position:

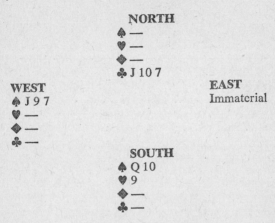

NORTH
♠ —
♥ —
♦ —
♣ J 10 7

WEST
♠ J 9 7
♥ —
♦ —
♣ —

EAST
Immaterial

SOUTH
♠ Q 10
♥ 9
♦ —
♣ —

A club lead from dummy and discard the heart. West ruffs and is forced to concede the last two tricks.

Once again the great Giorgio was right. And we were better prepared for the cold.

AVOIDING THE DANGEROUS DEFENDER
"Beard Beards Hamman"

Frank Beard, celebrated golfer and author of the much talked-about book "PRO—Frank Beard on the Golf Tour," likes to play serious bridge almost as well as he likes to sink birdie putts.

In the Byron Nelson Classic in Dallas, Beard managed a second place finish to go with his victory at the New Orleans Open the week before. In the pro-am, Beard played with Charles Weed, prominent Dallas bridge player, and after that, it was only natural that a friendly bridge foursome be arranged with The Aces.

Beard demonstrated admirable skill at the bridge table. Witness his accurate analysis and play of today's difficult game contract.

None vulnerable
Dealer South

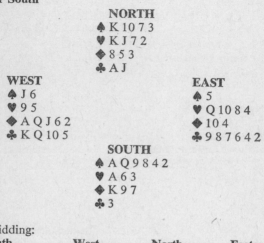

```
                      NORTH
                    ♠ K 10 7 3
                    ♥ K J 7 2
                    ◆ 8 5 3
                    ♣ A J
   WEST                              EAST
 ♠ J 6                             ♠ 5
 ♥ 9 5                             ♥ Q 10 8 4
 ◆ A Q J 6 2                       ◆ 10 4
 ♣ K Q 10 5                        ♣ 9 8 7 6 4 2
                      SOUTH
                    ♠ A Q 9 8 4 2
                    ♥ A 6 3
                    ◆ K 9 7
                    ♣ 3
```

The bidding:

South	West	North	East
1 ♠	2 ◆	3 ♠	Pass
4 ♠	Pass	Pass	Pass

Opening lead: King of clubs.

The bidding was routine, with Beard bidding the spade game after Ace Bob Hamman (West) overcalled in diamonds and Weed (North) made a jump raise in spades. The play did not prove as simple as the bidding.

As the cards were, many declarers would fail to make the contract. The bad lie of the hearts would prevent either a successful finesse in that suit or the establishment of a long heart for a vital diamond discard. A normal result would be down one, declarer losing three diamonds and one heart.

Alerted by the bidding and the opening lead, Beard found a

sure-fire way to land his contract.

Beard won the lead of the club king in dummy and drew trumps in two rounds. Beard then refused the heart finesse and played first his ace and then a low heart to dummy's king.

Next came dummy's club jack, and instead of ruffing, Beard discarded his remaining low heart. West was saddled with the lead and had no safe exits.

The lead of a diamond would establish Beard's king and the lead of a club would present Beard with a ruff and discard. (Note that even if West held one or more hearts, an unlikely event, dummy's heart jack could be established after a heart lead by West.)

Beard accepted the accolades modestly and graciously. "If only I had concentrated as hard on a few of those putts out there, I may have had a shot at the big prize."

There is no doubt about it; Frank Beard is quite a competitor.

END PLAY
"Lay It Down, Bud!"

Did you ever hear the story about the fellow who never lost an opportunity to peek into his opponents' hands? Unsuspecting opponents could not understand why he never lost a two-way finesse!

One day a shrewd lefthand opponent decided to cure the peeker's habit. He subtly exposed a singleton king of spades to the peeker, hiding his other spade with his clubs. Later, when the peeker was torn between bidding six or seven spades, the sight of the singleton king of spades convinced him to head for the rainbow. He bid seven spades.

After winning the first trick, declarer confidently banged down the ace of spades, only to catch a small one on his left. He was furious. He angrily announced that he was quitting, "never again to play in a game with such cheaters!"

Today's West heard about our story. Observe how he put it to use.

North-South vulnerable
Dealer East

                      NORTH
                      ♠ J
                      ♥ 2
                      ♦ A K 8 6 5
                      ♣ J 6 5 4 3 2
WEST
♠ A Q 8 2   EAST
♥ Q J 9 7 5 3   ♠ 10 9 7 5 3
♦ 4 3   ♥ 10 8 6 4
♣ K   ♦ J
                                       ♣ Q 10 9
                      SOUTH
                      ♠ K 6 4
                      ♥ A K
                      ♦ Q 10 9 7 2
                      ♣ A 8 7

The bidding:

East	South	West	North
Pass	1 ♦	2 ♦*	4 ♦
4 ♠	Dbl.	Pass	5 ♦
Pass	Pass	Pass	

*Michael's cue bid (major suits).
Opening lead: Ace of spades.

Opposite a Michael's cue bid, East reasoned that his double fit in the majors would ensure a cheap sacrifice if the opponents could make a game. East was right, and four spades would go down only one or two, depending upon the play and defense.

However, North decided to bid on, and now it was up to the defense. West got off to a good start by leading his ace of spades. Had he led anything else, South could have discarded dummy's losing spade on a high heart.

West decided to be cagey. He placed his king of clubs in with his spades, "accidentally" gave South a free peek, and then led the queen of hearts. South won, drew two rounds of trumps, ending in his hand. A high heart, the king of spades, and a spade ruff eliminated all major suit cards from South's hand and dummy.

A low club was played from dummy and, when East played the club 9, South ducked! West was finally on lead with his cherished king of clubs. But what could he play? He had only major-suit cards left, and all of these would yield a ruff and discard.

He finally decided on a heart. Declarer ruffed in dummy and discarded his losing club to make his contract.

Was there any defense to defeat the contract? Yes, but this particular West was not destined to find it. Instead of hiding the club king, West should have placed it on the table for all to see.

The only way to have defeated the contract was for West to have played his singleton king of clubs at trick two. With the club king gone, West could not be endplayed, and declarer would be forced to concede two clubs and a spade.

END PLAY
"In Trouble? Let Your Opponents Help You Out!"

Have you ever heard someone say about your local expert, "He seems to perform miracles when he is declarer. He takes more tricks with the same cards than anyone else in town."

What is the expert's secret?

Some of the more advanced plays are very complex and are better left in the world of the expert. However, many of the expert's secrets are available to and within the capabilities of the average player.

One of these secrets is the throw-in play. Here, the average player can easily join the expert. All that is needed is a study of fundamental principles and a desire to expend a reasonable amount of mental energy.

Today's hand was played by Lenny Schaen of Dallas. Study his technique in executing one of the more basic forms of the throw-in play.

None vulnerable
Dealer East

NORTH
- ♠ J 10 5
- ♥ A 10 3 2
- ♦ K Q 7
- ♣ Q 7 2

WEST
- ♠ Q 7 3
- ♥ Q 7 6
- ♦ 10 6 4 3
- ♣ 10 6 3

EAST
- ♠ A K 8 6 4
- ♥ 4
- ♦ J 8 5
- ♣ K 8 5 4

SOUTH
- ♠ 9 2
- ♥ K J 9 8 5
- ♦ A 9 2
- ♣ A J 9

The bidding:

East	South	West	North
1 ♠	Dbl.	Pass	2 ♠
Pass	3 ♥	Pass	4 ♥
Pass	Pass	Pass	

Opening lead: Three of spades.

The bidding was standard. Lenny's takeout double was superior to an overall call of two hearts because it left the door open to alternate contracts. North's cue bid said, "Partner, I have a very good hand. Tell me more about yours." The three-heart and four-heart bids were automatic.

East won the opening spade lead and continued spades for three rounds, Schaen ruffing. A heart to the ace and back to the king disclosed another trick for the defense. Declarer could afford to lose no more tricks.

Examine the club suit. If declarer plays clubs, he cannot keep from losing a trick. If the king is with East, East will cover the queen, promoting West's 10 to an eventual winner. If the king is with West, the hand cannot be made.

Declarer must hope for the club king to be with East. In addition, he must force the opponents to lead clubs or yield a ruff and discard. (If the K-10 of clubs are both with East, a double finesse will win. However, the throw-in is best, since it caters to the existing combination and does not lose to K-10 with East.)

Schaen played three rounds of diamonds, leaving West with no safe exit cards. When South placed West on lead with the heart queen, no defense could save him.

If West led a diamond, Lenny would ruff in dummy and discard his club 9. If West led a club, Lenny would win the club with his 9 and later finesse against the king. If the club suit were played in any other manner, Lenny could claim the balance.

PLAYING THE PERCENTAGES
"Gamble with the Odds in Your Favor"

All of The Aces are familiar with most of the important percentage plays and execute them more or less automatically. When an off-beat combination intrudes, then a player takes the time to work out the line of play most likely to succeed.

In today's example, let us examine how Ace Mike Lawrence and Sammy Kehela, internationally famous Canadian player, handled a combination more or less routinely but might provide a lesson for some of us. The hand was played in a challenge match between The Aces and a powerful squad headed by Edgar Kaplan.

East-West vulnerable
Dealer East

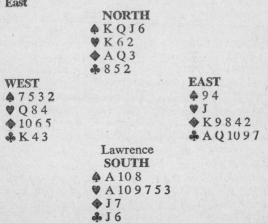

```
                    NORTH
                    ♠ K Q J 6
                    ♥ K 6 2
                    ♦ A Q 3
                    ♣ 8 5 2
        WEST                        EAST
        ♠ 7 5 3 2                   ♠ 9 4
        ♥ Q 8 4                     ♥ J
        ♦ 10 6 5                    ♦ K 9 8 4 2
        ♣ K 4 3                     ♣ A Q 10 9 7
                    Lawrence
                    SOUTH
                    ♠ A 10 8
                    ♥ A 10 9 7 5 3
                    ♦ J 7
                    ♣ J 6
```

The bidding:

East	South	West	North
Pass	Pass	Pass	1 ♠
Pass	2 ♥	Pass	3 ♥
Pass	4 ♥	Pass	Pass
Pass			

Opening lead: Three of clubs.

East won the club opening with the ace and returned the 9, his original fourth best. West took the king and shifted to a small diamond, and suddenly Lawrence had to fall back on his percentage tables to decide what to do.

He knew that if the hearts divided evenly, it would not matter whether he finessed diamonds or not, as the hand would be cold for ten tricks. However, assuming a trump loser, the problem became more complex.

Should Lawrence take the diamond finesse, a straight 50 percent chance? Or should he rise with the ace, play off two top trumps and start playing spades, hoping that the player with the outstanding high trump had at least three spades so that the diamond could be discarded on the fourth spade before that player could ruff in and cash a diamond?

Lawrence knew that the probability of a 3-3 spade division in the East-West hands was 36 percent and that a 4-2 division was 48 percent. So he added 36 percent to one-half of 48 percent (one-half the time the player with the outstanding trump would hold four spades) and came up with 60 percent.

This meant that he should be able to get rid of that jack of diamonds about 60 percent of the time by winning the diamond ace and playing on spades. Clearly a better proposition than a straight 50 percent chance on the diamond finesse.

So Lawrence rose with the ace of diamonds and played his two top trumps. When they did not divide, he worked on spades. Fortunately, the percentages did not let him down, and he was able to discard his losing diamond on the fourth spade as West watched helplessly, following to all four spades.

Unfortunately for The Aces, the Kaplan team also played the hand in four hearts in the other room, with Sammy Kehela of Toronto in the South position. Kehela apparently went to the same school (both declarers attended the University of California at Berkeley), as he also rose with the ace of diamonds and played the hand the same way for a standoff.

The Aces' tip for the day: When you have a combined holding of seven cards of a suit (your hand and the dummy),

the division of the outstanding six cards in the opponents'
hands is more likely to be uneven rather than even (4-2 rather than 3-3).

DEFENSIVE INFERENCE
"To Beat an Ace—Underplay One!"

The 1971 world championships were a hard-fought battle.
After France and The Aces had dominated the qualifying
rounds, and with France holding a slight edge in their head-
to-head meetings, the stage was set for the finals.

The Aces jumped off to a good lead after the initial 32-
board session even though the first 16 boards were very close
and low-scoring. The next two sessions were nip and tuck,
and only one international match point (IMP) was exchanged
after 64 grueling hands had been played in one day.

The early stages of the final session saw France make a
good dent into The Aces' lead. However, the French attack
ran out of gas, and in the final moments, The Aces increased
their margin to 61 IMPs.

The French team played well and fought back gamely on
three different occasions to reduce the Aces' margin uncom-
fortably.

Witness the exciting defense of today's hand, which thrilled
the audience watching the Vu-Graph presentation of the
match.

Both vulnerable
Dealer North

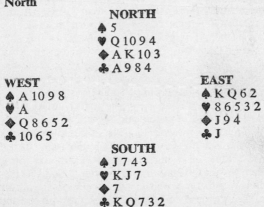

The bidding:

North	East	South	West
1 ♥	Pass	2 ♣	Pass
2 ♦	Pass	2 ♥	Pass
3 ♣	Pass	4 ♣	Pass
5 ♣	All pass		

Opening lead: Ace of hearts.

The results of the closed room, with the French pair holding the North-South cards, was good for The Aces. The French had reached a four-heart contract and, with the bad heart division, had gone down 300 points.

In the open room, Aces Jim Jacoby and Bobby Wolff reached the superior contract of five clubs, and if successful, would score a large gain for The Aces. Would the French find the killing defense?

Sitting West for France, Jean-Michel Boulenger, got off to the right start by selecting the heart ace as his opening lead. His partner, Henri Svarc, knew from the bidding that his partner's ace was a singleton. His problem was how to signal his entry in spades (assuming his partner held the ace).

After some thought, while the audience waited impatiently, East decided to play the heart deuce. He reasoned that a high heart would be read as holding the heart king rather than a suit preference signal for the higher-ranking side suit—spades. A very refined distinction.

Boulenger (West) read the situation perfectly and lost no time in underleading his spade ace. Svarc (East) gratefully won the queen and gave partner a ruff to defeat the contract.

This defense, while gaining less than was lost in the other room, prevented a very large loss at a critical stage. Full marks to a strong and gallant French team.

SQUEEZE PLAY
"A Hug From a Friend of Benjamin"

Bobbie Gentry, beautiful star of television and stage, famous for her record, "Ode To Billy Joe," has many and diversified talents. Aside from music composition and lyrics, she is first and foremost a writer and her house is a painting showcase—her own. A recent success is her album "Patchwork," for which she did the writing, performing and producing as well as the drawings and printed lyrics on the poster insert.

She also finds time for a little bridge.

Witness how careful play of today's slam deal resulted in another success story for Bobbie Gentry.

Both vulnerable
Dealer South

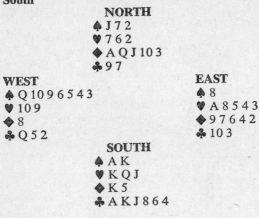

```
                    NORTH
                    ♠ J 7 2
                    ♥ 7 6 2
                    ♦ A Q J 10 3
                    ♣ 9 7
      WEST                          EAST
      ♠ Q 10 9 6 5 4 3              ♠ 8
      ♥ 10 9                        ♥ A 8 5 4 3
      ♦ 8                           ♦ 9 7 6 4 2
      ♣ Q 5 2                       ♣ 10 3
                    SOUTH
                    ♠ A K
                    ♥ K Q J
                    ♦ K 5
                    ♣ A K J 8 6 4
```

The bidding:

South	West	North	East
3 NT	Pass	6 NT	Pass
All pass			

Opening lead: Ten of hearts.

The bidding was quickly over. Miss Gentry opened with three no-trump, holding 24 high-card points and additional values in her six-card club suit. North had an easy raise to six no-trump, although it turned out that six diamonds would have been a better contract.

West opened the heart 10, won by East's ace and a heart return was won by Miss Gentry.

Eleven top tricks were immediately available and either of the black jacks was a potential candidate for the twelfth.

After winning the heart return, Miss Gentry cashed her two high spades, hoping to drop a doubleton queen. When this failed to materialize, she cashed a high club and a high heart. She noted that West had started with a doubleton heart.

The king of diamonds and a low diamond to dummy gave Miss Gentry a complete picture of both hands.

East had started with only one spade, was marked with five

hearts and five diamonds (West had shown out), and therefore he could hold only two clubs.

Having discovered this, the rest was easy. Either East had a doubleton queen of clubs and the hand would be easy, or if West had the club queen he would not be able to discard on the play of the last diamond. West would either have to discard the spade queen to establish dummy's jack or would have to unguard the queen of clubs.

Dummy's menacing spade jack forced West to discard a nonchalant club on the last diamond. However, Miss Gentry had made up her mind and took the last three tricks with the ace, king and jack of clubs.

A girl of many talents. And modest, too. She accepted her compliments thusly, "Well, actually all I did was note who showed out of what suits to count East's distribution!"

Talented? Yes, indeed!

KEY TO THE WINKLE
"Eat Your Heart Out"

Slams are the most exciting of bridge hands. The element of time assumes great importance, and an unfortunate choice of a lead can easily mean disaster.

Observe how Mervin Key of Houston, holding South's cards, executed a rare play to score a no-trump slam after the opponents failed to lead the suit in which they held two top tricks:

All vulnerable
Dealer South

```
                     NORTH
                     ♠ A K 7
                     ♥ J 7 5 2
                     ♦ K Q 9 5 2
                     ♣ K
    WEST                              EAST
    ♠ 10 5 4 3                       ♠ 9 8 2
    ♥ K 6                            ♥ A 8 4 3
    ♦ 10 8 7 6                       ♦ J 3
    ♣ 8 6 3                          ♣ 9 5 4 2
                     SOUTH
                     ♠ Q J 6
                     ♥ Q 10 9
                     ♦ A 4
                     ♣ A Q J 10 7
```

52

The bidding:

South	West	North	East
1 NT	Pass	2 ◆	Pass
2 NT	Pass	3 ◆	Pass
3 NT	Pass	6 NT	Pass
Pass	Pass		

Opening lead: Three of spades.

North's two-diamond bid was a specialized form of the Stayman convention, which forced to game. When South could show no biddable major suit and could not raise diamonds, North placed the final contract at six no-trump.

If West had led a heart, there would be no story to tell. However, if he had led a heart on this hand and on this bidding, maybe there would have been a story after all—one concerning the proprieties of East and West.

After West's lead of the spade three, declarer's chances remained alive, but the bad diamond distribution limited him to eleven top tricks, one short of the slam.

Declarer won the lead in dummy with the spade king, cashed the club king, and crossed to his hand with a low spade. On the run of his good clubs, declarer wisely gave up his chances to make all thirteen tricks and discarded one of dummy's low diamonds to keep the heart jack in dummy. After the run of the clubs, the position was:

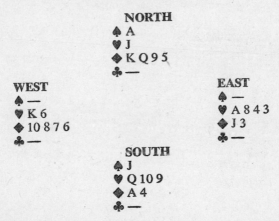

NORTH
♠ A
♥ J
◆ K Q 9 5
♣ —

WEST
♠ —
♥ K 6
◆ 10 8 7 6
♣ —

EAST
♠ —
♥ A 8 4 3
◆ J 3
♣ —

SOUTH
♠ J
♥ Q 10 9
◆ A 4
♣ —

When declarer led the spade jack to dummy's ace, West was forced to blank his heart king, since a diamond discard

53

would be fatal. The ace of diamonds and a diamond to dummy's queen dropped East's jack and placed Key at the crossroads. If diamonds were evenly divided, he could make twelve tricks by continuing the suit.

However, Key read the position accurately and, instead of playing for diamonds to divide evenly, led dummy's jack of hearts to demolish the defense. If East won the ace, he would have been forced to concede the last two hearts to declarer. If West won the king, he would have been forced to concede the last two diamonds to dummy.

What was the name of Key's unusual and rare play? It is called The Winkle. Maybe he'll get another one to score a slam after he sleeps on this one for twenty years.

FINESSING WINS
"If Spades Are Played, Your Chances Fade"

The 1971 world championship produced many hands that Mr. and Mrs. Bridge Player might well deal at home. While championship play might be more advanced, an occasional hand comes along that offers one of two choices—just like any simple deal at home.

Today's hand is such a hand. Both the French and The Aces played a contract of three no-trump from the South position. The French declarer chose one course while Ace Bobby Goldman chose another.

Decide on your play before reading about actual events at the table.

North-South vulnerable
Dealer South

```
                    NORTH
                    ♠ Q J 10 7 4
                    ♥ A
                    ♦ 7 6 5 3 2
                    ♣ Q 5
    WEST                                EAST
    ♠ 2                                 ♠ A 9 8 6 3
    ♥ 9 8 3 2                           ♥ 7 6 5
    ♦ 10 8 4                            ♦ K 9
    ♣ A J 9 7 3                         ♣ 10 6 4
                    SOUTH
                    ♠ K 5
                    ♥ K Q J 10 4
                    ♦ A Q J
                    ♣ K 8 2
```

The bidding:

South	West	North	East
1 ♥	Pass	1 ♠	Pass
2 NT	Pass	3 ♦	Pass
3 ♥	Pass	3 NT	Pass
Pass	Pass		

Opening lead: Seven of clubs.

When Aces Mike Lawrence and Bobby Goldman held the North-South cards, the bidding went as shown. West opened his fourth-best club and dummy's queen held the first trick. How do you play?

After much thought, Goldman decided to go after diamonds rather than spades. He led a diamond from dummy, intending to finesse. However, Goldman saw nine quick tricks when East rose with the diamond king in hopes of holding the trick and preserving partner's presumed diamond ace for later entry. Goldman took five hearts, three diamonds and one club to score his contract.

At the other table, Roger Trezel of Paris played the same contract against the same opening lead. Trezel also won the first trick with dummy's club queen.

Instead of playing diamonds, Trezel attacked the spade suit. Sitting East, Ace Bobby Wolff rose with the spade ace to lead clubs, and declarer went down to defeat.

Which line of play did you adopt?

If you chose the winning line, as did Bobby Goldman, you not only scored the contract but also made the best mathematical play.

If you chose the play made by Roger Trezel, you can console yourself with the fact that Trezel has played in four world championships. His play of today's hand, although not his best, is not so farfetched as to be considered a bad play.

THE MERRIMAC COUP
"Exercising the Queen's Prerogative"

One of the most unusual plays in bridge is known as the "Merrimac Coup." The play is named after the battle of 1862 that altered the course of naval warfare (Monitor vs. Merrimac, Hampton Roads, Va., March 9, 1862). For the bridge player, its effect on the course of the play of a hand is just as striking.

The Merrimac Coup, sometimes confused with the Deschapelles Coup, involves the deliberate sacrifice of a high card with the object of knocking out a vital entry in an opponent's hand, usually the dummy.

Witness an example of the Merrimac Coup executed by Ace Jim Jacoby in a hand played in the Mid-Atlantic Bridge Week tournament recently.

All vulnerable
Dealer North

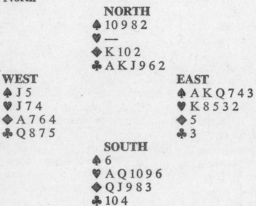

NORTH
♠ 10 9 8 2
♥ —
♦ K 10 2
♣ A K J 9 6 2

WEST
♠ J 5
♥ J 7 4
♦ A 7 6 4
♣ Q 8 7 5

EAST
♠ A K Q 7 4 3
♥ K 8 5 3 2
♦ 5
♣ 3

SOUTH
♠ 6
♥ A Q 10 9 6
♦ Q J 9 8 3
♣ 10 4

The bidding:

North	Wolff East	South	Jacoby West
1 ♣	2 ♣*	2 ♦	Pass
3 ♦	3 ♠	5 ♦	Dbl.
Pass	Pass	Pass	

*Major suit takeout.
Opening lead: Jack of spades.

Wolff's immediate cue bid described a hand with both major suits and asked Jacoby to bid his best major. Since South knew that Wolff had length in hearts, South suppressed his heart suit and bid two diamonds.

The rest of the bidding, though aggressive, was reasonable, since it was based on good distributional values.

Jacoby opened the jack of spades and continued the suit when he held the trick. South ruffed and led trumps. Jacoby refused to take the ace until the third round, waiting until dummy's trumps were exhausted. This was his first key play of the hand.

The second key play of the hand followed quickly. The queen of clubs! Jacoby deliberately sacrificed his queen of clubs to destroy the communication between the North and South hands. The Merrimac Coup.

If declarer won the club, the club 10 was the only entry to declarer's hand to extract Jacoby's last trump. If declarer did this, then he would have no entry to dummy's clubs after extracting Jacoby's trump. Truly an exasperating situation.

Note that Jacoby must refuse to take the trump ace until dummy is exhausted of trumps. Otherwise, declarer can gain entry to his hand in the trump suit. Declarer can then exhaust trumps and use his second club as an entry to dummy.

Note further that a low club lead by Jacoby also will fail. Declarer will allow the club to ride to his 10, extract the trump and take another club finesse to make his contract.

PARTNERSHIP DISCIPLINE
"Woodsman, Spare That Treyl"

Discipline is the main quality that separates near-expert players from their cousin, the polished expert.

Discipline is defined as the ability of both members of a partnership to follow an agreed system when partnership action is called for. It requires not only the ability to subordinate one's individual desires and bias; it also demands complete confidence and respect of one's partner. Which is why it is such a scarce commodity.

Today's hand demonstrates discipline in both bidding and play.

North-South vulnerable
Dealer East

                          NORTH
                          ♠ A 10 5 2
                          ♥ J 6
                          ♦ K J 7 5
                          ♣ 10 9 2

        WEST   **EAST**
        ♠ 3   ♠ 6
        ♥ A 7 3   ♥ K Q 10 9 8 5 4 2
        ♦ A 10 9 6 4 2   ♦ 3
        ♣ 8 7 6   ♣ J 5 4

                          SOUTH
                          ♠ K Q J 9 8 7 4
                          ♥ —
                          ♦ Q 8
                          ♣ A K Q 3

The bidding:

East	South	West	North
4 ♥	4 ♠	5 ♥	5 ♠
Pass	6 ♠	Pass	Pass
Pass			

Opening lead: Ace of hearts.

At favorable vulnerability, East's preemptive four-heart
bid is approved modern practice. South's four-spade bid,
West's five-heart bid and North's five-spade bid are all reasonable actions in light of the extreme lack of exploratory space
caused by the preemptive auction.

South decided to gamble a slam, hoping that partner had
the right cards. West passed six spades, hoping to defeat the
contract but not sure enough to double.

East's pass was a fine example of partnership discipline. He
knew that a seven-heart sacrifice would not cost much, but he
also realized that if the sacrifice were warranted, it was West's
decision to make and not his.

West opened the ace of diamonds. Dummy and East followed with the five and three. Declarer, in an effort to mislead
West, dropped the queen on the ace.

West's next play would make a difference of some 1,500
points! As the reader can see, if West attempted to cash the
heart ace, declarer would ruff and easily score his contract.

West showed complete discipline and confidence in partner

by continuing diamonds instead of attempting to cash the heart ace.

West reasoned as follows: If declarer had truly held a singleton queen of diamonds, then East would have started with the 8 and 3 of diamonds. If this had been so, East's proper play to the first trick was the diamond 8 and not the 3! Since West had complete trust in his partner to make the correct play, he was able to conclude that East had the singleton 2.

What about declarer's play?

It was a futile attempt at false-carding and succeeded only in making things easy for West. Note that if declarer had followed with the diamond 8, West might well have tried to cash the heart ace, playing East for an original holding of Q-3 of diamonds.

THE FAULTY HOLDUP
"The Grave's a Fine and Quiet Place,
But No One There Will Cash His Ace"

Today's hand was played in a recent duplicate game. The variations in play and defense were the subject of some discussion. Study all four hands and make a mental wager on either the declarer or the defense.

Can the hand be made, or must it go down to defeat?

North-South vulnerable
Dealer South

```
                    NORTH
                    ♠ 10 9 8
                    ♥ Q J 10 9
                    ♦ A 10 8 2
                    ♣ 6 3

   WEST                              EAST
   ♠ K J 7 2                         ♠ 6 5 4
   ♥ 7 4                             ♥ A 6 3 2
   ♦ J 9 6                           ♦ 7 3
   ♣ J 8 5 4                         ♣ K Q 9 7

                    SOUTH
                    ♠ A Q 3
                    ♥ K 8 5
                    ♦ K Q 5 4
                    ♣ A 10 2
```

The bidding:

South	West	North	East
1 ♦	Pass	1 ♥	Pass
2 NT	Pass	3 NT	Pass
Pass	Pass		

Opening lead: Four of clubs.

North-South were playing 15-17 point opening no-trumps, which explains South's rebid of two no-trump. North was happy to raise to game.

West dodged the disastrous spade lead and led the club 4. East played the queen and South refused the trick, playing his deuce.

East continued with the club king, which South ducked again, and East cleared the suit. Declarer knocked out the heart ace and then took his top tricks for his contract—one spade, three hearts, four diamonds and one club.

West said, "If you had shifted to a spade at trick two, we would have defeated the hand."

East agreed, "Yes, I had two chances to do so. I could have also done so after winning the second club."

South entered the discussion with, "If you had shifted to spades, I would have played low, allowing West to win his jack. However, he could not continue the attack on spades."

West countered, "I would have returned to the attack on the club suit and we would have taken one spade, three clubs and a heart."

Who do you bet on, the declarer or the defense?

If you bet on the defense, you were wrong—unless, of course, you can force South to duck the first club. Assuming West's lead to be a true fourth best, South should have taken the first club trick. Dislodging the heart ace would have limited his losses to three clubs and one heart.

South's "automatic" duck gave the defense a chance, and he was fortunate that East did not find the winning defense.

WHEN TO LEAD TRUMPS
"Be Analytic—Not Bromidic"

When in doubt, lead trumps. How many times have you heard this advice? Does it have any validity?

This bromide, like many other bridge clichés, probably was

offered first to a beginning bridge player who, in his early stage of development, could remember and apply only general rules. For him, it really isn't bad advice.

If no clear reason exists to lead a suit, then a trump lead may be best, since it is less likely to give away a trick. The theory, about equal in validity to the cliché, is that declarer probably has most of the trumps anyway.

For the more sophisticated player, analysis of the bidding will usually guide the way to an effective trump lead.

Witness the defense of today's hand.

None vulnerable
Dealer North

```
                    NORTH
                    ♠ A 9 3
                    ♥ 7
                    ♦ A 10 7 3 2
                    ♣ A K 8 7
WEST                                EAST
♠ 7 5 2                             ♠ K 4
♥ K J 5 4                           ♥ A 9 3
♦ 9 6                               ♦ Q J 8 5 4
♣ J 10 6 5                          ♣ 9 3 2
                    SOUTH
                    ♠ Q J 10 8 6
                    ♥ Q 10 8 6 2
                    ♦ K
                    ♣ Q 4
```

The bidding:

North	East	South	West
1 ♦	Pass	1 ♠	Pass
2 ♣	Pass	2 ♠	Pass
4 ♠	Pass	Pass	Pass

Opening lead: Two of spades.

Why South chose to rebid two spades rather than two hearts will remain a mystery forever. Maybe South had *two* of his hearts in with his diamonds!

West, Sam Beard of Dallas, decided to lead a trump. Why? North's bidding revealed shortness in hearts because he had bid both minors and then jumped to four spades. Clearly, South was going to use dummy's trumps to ruff his heart losers. A good time to lead trumps!

Declarer ducked in dummy and East won the king. East re-

61

turned his last trump, taken by dummy's 9. Dummy's single-ton heart was played and, since East had no more trumps to lead, he made the excellent play of ducking the ace.

South played the heart 10 won by West's jack. Beard re-turned his last trump, which prevented South from ruffing any hearts in dummy.

This excellent defense defeated the contract. All South needed was one heart ruff in dummy to add to his four spades, two diamonds and three clubs. He didn't get it.

Note that any other lead would have enabled South to ruff at least one heart in dummy. Good analysis of the bidding by Beard, rather than "when in doubt . . ." guided him to the winning lead.

Keen analysts may have already noticed that South would have made his contract had he made the unusual play of the spade ace at trick one. A heart is led at trick two, and re-gardless of which defender wins, the spades are so divid-ed so as to prevent the defenders from clearing the trumps. South could then use one of dummy's trumps to ruff a heart.

BRILLIANT DEFENSE
"Think Before You Play"

In S. J. Simon's classic work, "Why You Lose at Bridge," he had this to say about defense:

"To become the perfect defensive player at bridge, you will need a combination of logic and flair. You must be sound or brilliant as the occasion demands. You must be able to draw the right inferences from the bidding, visualize all possibilities to select the most promising, and grasp what declarer is trying to do, often before he attempts to do it. On top of this you will still need perfect partnership cooperation.

"Which makes the whole thing impossible."

Consider the play of today's hand.

No one vulnerable
Dealer South

                         NORTH
                    ♠ K 10 5 3
                    ♥ J 8 6 3
                    ♦ A K 5
                    ♣ 10 3

    WEST   EAST
    ♠ 7 6   ♠ 9 8 2
    ♥ 7   ♥ A Q 10 9
    ♦ Q 9 6 4 3 2   ♦ 7
    ♣ Q 9 7 2   ♣ K J 6 5 4

                         SOUTH
                    ♠ A Q J 4
                    ♥ K 5 4 2
                    ♦ J 10 8
                    ♣ A 8

The bidding:

South	West	North	East
1 ♠	Pass	3 ♠*	Pass
4 ♠	Pass	Pass	Pass

*Limit raise indicating 10-12 points.
 Opening lead: Seven of hearts

   West's opening lead was his singleton heart. East won with
the ace and returned the 9. Declarer analyzed the situation
properly and played low, West ruffing the trick.
   A club was led and declarer won with the ace. After two
rounds of trumps, declarer first cashed dummy's diamond ace
before returning to his hand with a third round of trumps. He
now took the successful diamond finesse, cashed the diamond
king and exited with a club. This was now the position:

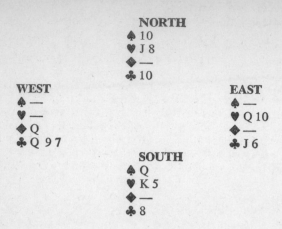

NORTH
♠ 10
♥ J 8
♦ —
♣ 10

WEST
♠ —
♥ —
♦ Q
♣ Q 9 7

EAST
♠ —
♥ Q 10
♦ —
♣ J 6

SOUTH
♠ Q
♥ K 5
♦ —
♣ 8

East-West were in an impossible situation. If West won the club trick, he would be forced to lead a minor suit. Declarer would ruff and discard a heart for his tenth trick.

However, if East were allowed to win the club trick, he would be forced to either concede a ruff and discard or to provide a marked finesse in the heart suit.

Declarer played the hand well. He succeeded in an "elimination" play. Dummy's and declarer's side suits (diamonds and clubs) were eliminated, making it impossible for the defense to make a lead without sacrificing a trick.

How about the defense?

After the first two tricks the defense could only follow suit or revoke. Nothing wrong happened there. Examine East's heart return at trick two.

What would happen if he had returned the heart *queen?* Declarer would have been helpless! If he ducked, the queen would win the trick and another heart led and ruffed. If he covered the heart queen with the king, West would ruff. Later, when declarer exited with a club, the elimination play would fail because East could win declarer's club exit and make the safe return of the heart 10. Declarer would be forced to lose one club and three heart tricks regardless of which course he chose.

See what S. J. Simon meant?

DISCARD WAS THE KEY
"One Man's Trash Is Another Man's Treasure"

The Aces' margin of victory set a record in winning the Vanderbilt National Knockout Team Championship in March. In doing so, The Aces became strong favorites to represent the United States in the 1972 World Team Olympiad.

The Aces won the Vanderbilt final match by 156 international match points (IMPs), the largest margin ever in a national knockout final. A series of slam disasters for the losers in the first quarter of play helped give The Aces a mammoth 97-1 lead to virtually salt the match away.

Today's hand is one of the slam deals that swung 29 IMPs to The Aces.

North-South vulnerable
Dealer East

```
                    NORTH
                    ♠ K J 9
                    ♥ K J 4 2
                    ♦ K 9 4
                    ♣ A J 5
     WEST                             EAST
     ♠ Q 10 5                         ♠ 6 4 3
     ♥ Q 10 9 7 3                     ♥ 8
     ♦ 10                             ♦ J 6 5
     ♣ K 9 8 6                        ♣ Q 10 7 4 3 2
                    SOUTH
                    ♠ A 8 7 2
                    ♥ A 6 5
                    ♦ A Q 8 7 3 2
                    ♣ —
```

The bidding:

East	South	West	North
Pass	1 ◆	Pass	3 NT
Pass	4 ◆	Pass	5 ♣
Pass	5 NT	Pass	6 ◆
Pass	7 ◆	Pass	Pass

Opening lead: Ten of diamonds

The bidding was standard, with North's three no-trump bid promising an opening no-trump bid and his five-club bid showing the club ace. South's five no-trump was the Grand

65

Slam Force, asking about North's trump honors. North's response of six diamonds showed one high honor (in their methods), and South optimistically bid the grand slam.

After the lead of the diamond 10 was won by declarer's ace, declarer led a trump to dummy's king and discarded a heart on dummy's club ace. Declarer could make his contract easily if he decided to take a simple finesse against West's queen. Almost anyone reading this column would make the contract by taking a deep breath and finessing the spade.

However, this day belonged to The Aces and declarer went astray. He ruffed one of dummy's clubs and then drew the last trump. Ace Billy Eisenberg, sitting West, discarded the spade 5 and the club 9 on the second and third round of trumps.

Eisenberg's spade discard created the impression that the spade queen might be with East. This key card could then be captured via a finesse if West had started with a doubleton or tripleton 10.

After cashing his two high hearts, declarer played dummy's spade king, and when the 10 fell from West, he followed with the jack and finessed against East. Eisenberg gratefully accepted the queen to defeat the contract one trick.

Eisenberg's clever discarding helped gain 16 IMPs instead of losing 13 IMPs. His teammates, Jim Jacoby and Bobby Wolff, in the other room, had played the reasonable and comfortable small slam.

The Vanderbilt Cup was a first for The Aces and gave them the distinction of winning every major United States bridge title at least once.

THE RIGHT PLAY AT THE WRONG TIME
"Why We Palookas Can Sometimes Cash an Expert's Check"

William B. Tanner, president of Pepper and Tanner, Inc., is also the president of the Colonial Country Club of Memphis, hosts of the annual Danny Thomas Open Golf Tournament.

Tanner sometimes demonstrates he can also "run things" at the bridge table. Witness his defense of today's exciting deal. Tanner held West's cards.

Both vulnerable
Dealer East

                        NORTH
                        ♠ K 9 7 4 3
                        ♥ Q 10 6 2
                        ◆ K 8 3
                        ♣ 3

        WEST   EAST
        ♠ Q 8 5 2   ♠ A 10
        ♥ A 7   ♥ K J 9 8 5 4 3
        ◆ 10 9 2   ◆ J
        ♣ 10 7 6 2   ♣ Q 5 4

                        SOUTH
                        ♠ J 6
                        ♥ —
                        ◆ A Q 7 6 5 4
                        ♣ A K J 9 8

The bidding:

East	South	West	North
3 ♥	4 ◆	Pass	5 ◆
Pass	Pass	Pass	

Opening lead: Ace of hearts.

Over East's preemptive bid of three hearts, South chose his longer minor suit and was quickly raised to game.

Tanner led the ace of hearts and, after seeing four hearts in dummy, had little hope of winning the trick. Declarer ruffed and Tanner's suspicions were confirmed.

Declarer led a low spade to dummy's king and East's ace. East returned the 10 of spades, Tanner won the queen and paused for study. Did the defense have a trick in clubs to set the contract? Hardly.

East had opened a preemptive three hearts and had already shown seven hearts, headed by K-J, and the ace of spades. Any more high cards and he surely would not have made a preemptive bid.

Tanner reasoned his only hope lay in an uppercut. If East held any diamond honor, another spade lead would finish South. Accordingly, he led a third round of spades and East obliged with the jack of trumps. This dislodged one of South's high honors and promoted Tanner's diamond holding to a sure trick.

As the cards lie, declarer could have made the hand by leading one round of trumps (to the king) before playing spades. Alternately, he could have played for a favorable club position.

Declarer chose neither, since he didn't want a second trump continued after the defense won the spade ace and he, justifiably, wanted to find out about spades before playing clubs.

Declarer was unlucky. In choosing a reasonable line of play he gave Tanner a chance to find the winning defense. Few declarers have been lucky against Bill Tanner in these situations.

ELIMINATE BASIC ERRORS
"Only an Expert Could Go Wrong"

In relating one of his bridge experiences, Jim Jacoby said, "I learned my first bridge from an optimistic teacher, my father. He advised, 'If you apply yourself diligently and study hard, you will be able to eliminate all basic errors.'

"I learned later he was right. In time, my basic errors just about disappeared. However, you should see some of my advanced ones!"

Jim was the goat in today's hand. Mainly because he is thorough in analysis. Witness his reward for diligence on the following deal:

East-West vulnerable
Dealer South

```
                  NORTH
                  ♠ Q J 2
                  ♥ K 10 7 4 2
                  ♦ 10 3
                  ♣ K 10 8
   WEST                            EAST
   ♠ 10 4                          ♠ A 7 6 5 3
   ♥ 9                             ♥ 6 3
   ♦ J 9 6 5 2                     ♦ K Q 7 4
   ♣ A Q 9 5 2                     ♣ 7 6
                  SOUTH
                  ♠ K 9 8
                  ♥ A Q J 8 5
                  ♦ A 8
                  ♣ J 4 3
```

The bidding:

South	West	North	East
1 ♥	Pass	3 ♥*	Pass
4 ♥	Pass	Pass	Pass

*Limit raise indicating 10-12 points.
Opening lead: Five of diamonds.

Jim won the first trick, capturing East's queen of diamonds with his ace. Two rounds of trumps followed, West discarding the diamond deuce. Jim now played spades. East took dummy's queen, cashed the king of diamonds and exited with a spade. Jim cashed both spades, West discarding a club.

The position was now as follows, and Jim would make his contract if he could hold his losses to one club trick. (As the reader can see, this is easily done by finessing against West's queen.)

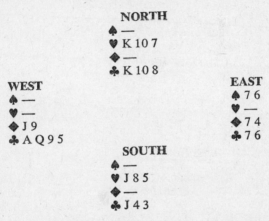

```
                        NORTH
                        ♠ —
                        ♥ K 10 7
                        ♦ —
                        ♣ K 10 8

        WEST                            EAST
        ♠ —                             ♠ 7 6
        ♥ —                             ♥ —
        ♦ J 9                           ♦ 7 4
        ♣ A Q 9 5                       ♣ 7 6

                        SOUTH
                        ♠ —
                        ♥ J 8 5
                        ♦ —
                        ♣ J 4 3
```

At this crucial point Jim led the club jack, hoping to find some clue in West's reaction. West unflinchingly followed low.

Before selecting his play, Jim reconstructed the entire hand. Apparently East had started with five spades to the ace, two small hearts, four diamonds to the K-Q (based upon West's discarding in the diamond suit) and therefore only two clubs.

Jim wondered, "If East held the club ace, would he have passed over three hearts?" Probably not. Therefore, East's two clubs did not include the ace but might include the queen.

One step further. If East held two small clubs, West would

have the ace and queen. Could West hold both and follow to the club jack with no apparent thought or concern? (See how difficult it is to talk yourself into making an advanced error?)

His analysis over, Jim assumed East held Q-x in clubs, rendering the club finesse futile. So he played the club king and a low club to East's imagined queen. If East had held the queen, East-West would be helpless. If East won the queen, he would be forced to concede a ruff and discard. If West "rescued" by overtaking with his ace, dummy's 10 would become a winner.

When West innocently cashed both his ace and queen to defeat the contract, Jim couldn't help but recall his early bridge errors. "Why did I have to study so hard?" he thought. "Twenty years ago I would not have known enough to go set."

UNUSUAL LEAD PAYS OFF FOR DEFENSE
"Doin' What Come Unnaturally!"

The 1971 world championship was played in Taipei, Taiwan, in May. Two teams will represent North America. The Aces, as defenders of their 1970 world title, will be one.

Four Los Angeles players, Lew Mathe, Don Krauss, Richard Walsh and John Swanson, won a series of elimination matches to earn the right to become the other North American team. They have invited Edgar Kaplan of New York City and Norman Kay of Philadelphia to join their team for world championship play.

In a recent national tournament, Mathe and Kaplan played together in a men's pair event. Mathe is known for his aggressive style, while Kaplan tends to have more count for the same bids. Witness the fireworks on today's hand when the different styles managed to reach a small slam while missing two aces.

70

East-West vulnerable
Dealer East

NORTH
♠ A K 10 8 2
♥ K 10 7 4
♦ J 7 5 3
♣ —

WEST
♠ Q 9 3
♥ A J 6 5 3
♦ —
♣ K 9 8 7 6

EAST
♠ J 6 4
♥ Q 9 2
♦ A 10
♣ Q J 10 3 2

SOUTH
♠ 7 5
♥ 8
♦ K Q 9 8 6 4 2
♣ A 5 4

The bidding:

East	South	West	North
Pass	1 ♦	1 ♥	1 ♠
2 ♥	3 ♦	3 ♥	6 ♦
Dbl.	Pass	Pass	Pass

Opening lead: Three of spades.

Needless to say, Kaplan (North) thought that Mathe (South) had more values for his opening bid and his free rebid of three diamonds. That explains Kaplan's jump to six diamonds over three hearts.

East's double was based on his trump ace, general strength and his partner's overcall. He was right in that he could beat the hand. However, some strange things were about to happen.

West interpreted East's double of the slam as a request for an unusual lead (the Lighter Slam Double) and led the spade three. This was all the help that Mathe needed.

Mathe won the spade in dummy, cashed another high spade and ruffed a third spade to establish the suit. Dummy was entered with a club ruff and a winning spade was led.

Since declarer could discard his losing heart if East failed to ruff (or if East ruffed with the ace), East ruffed with his diamond 10. Declarer overruffed, returned to dummy with another club ruff and led another good spade. Whether East ruffed or not, declarer threw his losing heart and claimed the slam.

At the tournament, this hand received some eyebrow-raising publicity, with emphasis on Mathe's penchant for bidding. However, as the result shows, Mathe had the last laugh, since he made his contract. It was another one of Mathe's trademarks—bringing home the impossible contract.

A TEAM'S DREAM
"Steve Loses Steam"

Most experienced tournament competitors prefer to play in team contests. The theory is that much of the unpredictability of luck is minimized and that the good play or the good result is usually rewarded.

Unfortunately, as in all other phases of bridge, around every corner lurks the exception to prove the rule.

Observe how Steve Altman of New York City, captain of the team that won the 1970 Spingold Tournament, fared when he beat the opponents three tricks in a contract that was doubled, redoubled and vulnerable.

Both vulnerable
Dealer West

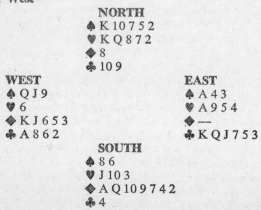

```
                    NORTH
                    ♠ K 10 7 5 2
                    ♥ K Q 8 7 2
                    ♦ 8
                    ♣ 10 9
    WEST                              EAST
    ♠ Q J 9                          ♠ A 4 3
    ♥ 6                              ♥ A 9 5 4
    ♦ K J 6 5 3                      ♦ —
    ♣ A 8 6 2                        ♣ K Q J 7 5 3
                    SOUTH
                    ♠ 8 6
                    ♥ J 10 3
                    ♦ A Q 10 9 7 4 2
                    ♣ 4
```

The bidding:

West	North	East	South
	Pass	1 ♣	2 ♦
Pass	Pass	1 ♣	2 ♦
Dbl.	Rdbl.	Pass	Pass
Pass			

Opening lead: Queen of spades.

A word about the bidding. Over East's opening of one club, South made a weak jump overcall of two diamonds (a modern treatment showing a weak hand but a good long suit). Altman, West, doubled for business.

North's redouble was intended as a request for South to choose another suit (an SOS). However, South decided to play in diamonds, since he had a seven-card suit with good texture.

The defense was merciless. The queen of spades was ducked by all, and West shifted to his singleton heart. East won and gave West a heart ruff. Another spade to the ace and another heart ruff. The ace of clubs and two more diamonds totaled eight defensive tricks and 1,600 points for Altman.

How could Altman possibly lose points on this deal? Although his side could make a small slam in clubs, East-West were unlikely to bid that high. If they did, that score would only be 1,370 points, and if doubled, only 1,540 points.

Naturally, Altman felt comfortable about his result. He could hardly foresee the results at the other table.

In the other room the bidding was:

West	North	East	South
Pass	1 ♠	2 ♠	Pass
4 ♣	Pass	5 ♣	5 ♦
Dbl.	Pass	Pass	Pass

After North's opening bid of one spade, East's cue bid showed six clubs and four hearts. South decided to await developments, and his next decision came at the five level. Unfortunately, he decided to bid five diamonds and was doubled.

The defense took the same eight tricks as at the other table —down six. Down six vulnerable totals 1,700 points—100 more than the previous result.

Altman consoled himself with the fact that his team lost the hand by a small margin—only 100 points of the total of 3,300 points scored at both tables.

"Go After Those Trumps"

Barry Crane, producer of the popular television series
"Mission Impossible," is one of the leading tournament
players in the country. Each year he is among the top finish-
ers for the McKenney Trophy, the annual award to the tournament player winning the largest number of master points
during the year.

Observe how Barry Crane (South) earned a fine score in
the play of today's game contract.

Both vulnerable
Dealer North

```
                    NORTH
                    ♠ J 7 6
                    ♥ A 10 7 4 2
                    ◆ 8 3
                    ♣ J 10 5
    WEST                              EAST
    ♠ K 10 9                         ♠ A 8
    ♥ 9 8 6 3                        ♥ 5
    ◆ Q 5 4                          ◆ A J 10 9 7 6 2
    ♣ Q 7 2                          ♣ 9 6 4
                    SOUTH
                    ♠ Q 5 4 3 2
                    ♥ K Q J
                    ◆ K
                    ♣ A K 8 3
```

The bidding:

North	East	South	West
Pass	Pass	1 ♠	Pass
2 ♠	3 ◆	4 ♠	Pass
Pass	Pass		

Opening lead: Four of diamonds.

Crane's consistent ability to score well in tournament competition is due to his aggressive bidding and excellent card
play. Today's hand demonstrates both of these hallmarks.

West's lead of the diamond 4 was won by East's ace, dropping Crane's king. The diamond continuation was ruffed by
declarer and the future was dim.

Declarer's problem was to find a method to limit the defense to only two trump tricks without using dummy's lone entry, the heart ace, for positional plays in the trump suit. The heart ace was needed to run the heart suit so that a club finesse need not be taken.

With lightning rapidity, Crane played the trump queen from his hand—the only play to make the contract! East won the ace and led a third diamond (as good as any other defense). Crane ruffed and led a spade toward dummy's jack and West was in a hopeless position.

If West took his king of trumps, he could not lead diamonds (another diamond lead would defeat the contract). If West ducked the trump king, Crane would continue with and eliminate all the spades, win any lead by West, and claim the contract.

Crane took three spades, five hearts and two clubs for ten tricks and his contract.

Note that any other play of the trump suit would fail. If Crane had led a low spade at trick three, East would have captured North's jack with the ace and West would be left with two spade tricks.

If Crane had led to dummy's heart ace to play spades from dummy, West could duck two spade leads and dummy would be without entry to the long hearts. Declarer would then be forced to concede a club trick for down one.

Believe it or not, East-West were neither dictators nor prime ministers of any foreign powers. However, they did get a first-hand glimpse of Crane's active imagination—another seemingly "mission impossible."

SLUFF AND RUFF HELPFUL TO DEFENSE
"Wishes Are Sweeter Than Wine"

The Fairy Godmother can sometimes grant our wishes. We must, however, be careful not to ask for too much. Small wishes are easier to grant than large ones—even for Fairy Godmothers.

Observe the difference in the wishes made by two different Wests in defense of today's game contract.

Both vulnerable
Dealer South

```
                    NORTH
                    ♠ K Q 5
                    ♥ 7 4 3
                    ◆ J 3
                    ♣ A K Q 10 9
        WEST                        EAST
        ♠ J 4                       ♠ 10 9 8 7 3
        ♥ A 9 5                     ♥ 10 6
        ◆ A K 8 7 5 2               ◆ 10 9 6
        ♣ 8 7                       ♣ 6 4 2
                    SOUTH
                    ♠ A 6 2
                    ♥ K Q J 8 2
                    ◆ Q 4
                    ♣ J 5 3
```

The bidding:

South	West	North	East
1 ♥	2 ◆	3 ♣	Pass
3 ♥	Pass	4 ♥	Pass
Pass	Pass		

Opening lead: King of diamonds.

The bidding was uneventful, and North-South reached the reasonable game contract in hearts.

Our first defender's opening lead was the king of diamonds. He followed with his ace, and when this held the trick, he made his wish. Since he had a third trick in the trump ace, he wished for a trick in spades to set the contract.

West led a spade in the hopes that East could win. However, declarer won with dummy's queen. Declarer played trumps and had no trouble scoring ten tricks and his contract. He lost only two diamonds and one heart.

When the hand was defended by George Healy, editor of the New Orleans Times-Picayune, he made a much smaller wish.

A look at dummy and a review of the bidding made it clear that a wish for East to have the spade ace was asking too much. Instead, Healy wished for partner to have either the jack or the 10 of hearts. Certainly a reasonable wish.

Healy also started with the king and ace of diamonds. At trick three, he continued with a third diamond! He knew this would afford declarer a sluff and ruff. He also knew that East held no high cards and a sluff and ruff wasn't going to give declarer anything he did not already have.

Declarer ruffed the third diamond in dummy and discarded a club. A heart was led from dummy, declarer played the jack and Healy won his ace. He continued with a fourth round of diamonds and declarer's goose was cooked when East ruffed with the 10.

Declarer had no choice and overruffed. This promoted Healy's trump 9 to a sure trick and the contract was defeated.

Like Healy, if you learn to keep your wishes within reason, your Fairy Godmother should be able to grant a few of them.

IMAGINATIVE DEFENSIVE PLAY
"The Dream Becomes a Nightmare"

Do you dream? Are your dreams in color?

No, we haven't mixed your horoscope forecast with the bridge column. Bridge players also have dreams. Bad ones . . . and in color, especially after a particularly trying session.

Billy Eisenberg of The Aces tells of one of his dreams. The dream came to him after a close match in which he had experienced considerable difficulty with the trump suit. To hear him tell it, he was the victim of every bad trump break ever invented. Bridge players just can't help a little exaggeration.

Let's turn on the brainwave analyzer and tune in on Billy's nightmare. He is sitting South.

North-South vulnerable
Dealer South

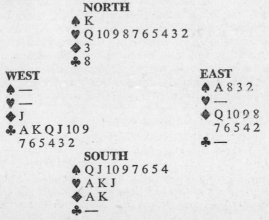

NORTH
♠ K
♥ Q 10 9 8 7 6 5 4 3 2
♦ 3
♣ 8

WEST
♠ —
♥ —
♦ J
♣ A K Q J 10 9
  7 6 5 4 3 2

EAST
♠ A 8 3 2
♥ —
♦ Q 10 9 8
  7 6 5 4 2
♣ —

SOUTH
♠ Q J 10 9 7 6 5 4
♥ A K J
♦ A K
♣ —

The bidding:

South	West	North	East
5 ♠	6 ♣	6 ♠	Dbl.
Pass	Pass	Pass	

Opening lead: Ace of clubs.

Billy's bid of five spades is a specialized bid first popularized by Ely Culbertson. It describes a solid hand outside the
trump suit and asks partner to raise one level for each of the
two top honors he might hold.

West bid six clubs in a feigned attitude of "I'm taking the
sacrifice, partner" (unethical behavior is obviously permissible in dreams). North dutifully raised to six spades, and East
doubled confidently. Sitting East was the same culprit who
had held all of Billy's trumps all evening.

West led the ace of clubs, and North meekly laid down the
dummy. When Billy saw dummy his eyes beamed and the first
smile of the day lit his face. "Now I'm going to get even with
you," he sneered.

Billy saw no way to go down. The opponents certainly
could not get a heart ruff when Billy surrendered the ace of
spades—they were both void! A diamond ruff was equally unlikely.

How did Billy's sweet dream turn into a nightmare? Did he
fall out of bed, or can you figure out what happened?

East ruffed the club ace with the *ace* of spades and led a
diamond! Billy won the diamond and led a spade to the king.
Dummy was reduced to only the heart suit and Billy was
stuck in dummy.

Billy led a low heart from dummy, and East triumphantly
ruffed. "Down one," cried East as Billy's nightmare unfolded
and our brainwave analyzer went up in smoke.

The following day Billy was heard saying, "The next time I
have a session with bad trump stacks, I'm making arrange-
ments for an all-night party." Who knows, dodging one of
these nightmares may be worth a $50 fine for breaking cur-
few?

THE SQUEEZE PLAY
"Pard, I Had to Play **Something** on That Last Trump"

Most of us find that a grand slam comes our way much too
infrequently. Even more infrequent is a grand slam after the
opponents open the bidding!

Observe how today's North-South pair bid and made a grand slam after an opening bid by the opponents. The deal was played in the Life Masters Men's Pair National Championship recently in Houston.

North-South vulnerable
Dealer South

                    NORTH
                    ♠ A K J 9
                    ♥ A K 7
                    ♦ K 9 8
                    ♣ K 5 2

    WEST   EAST
    ♠ Q 8 7   ♠ 6 4
    ♥ 6 3   ♥ Q 5
    ♦ A Q J 10 5   ♦ 7 6 4 3 2
    ♣ Q J 4   ♣ 9 8 7 6

                    SOUTH
                    ♠ 10 5 3 2
                    ♥ J 10 9 8 4 2
                    ♦ —
                    ♣ A 10 3

The bidding:

South	West	North	East
Pass	1 ♦	Dbl.	Pass
4 ♥	Pass	4 NT	Pass
6 ♦	Pass	7 ♥	Pass
Pass	Pass		

Opening lead: Three of hearts.

West's decision to open the bidding with his super-light hand served to aid the opponents rather than hinder them. Over North's takeout double, South chose the aggressive bid of four hearts. This goaded North into a Blackwood bid, and South's response of six diamonds showed one ace and a void in the diamond suit.

This was all that North needed to push him further, and so he bid the grand slam. He reasoned that the spade queen should be finessable and that thirteen tricks would be available if South had a seven-card suit.

After the lead of the heart three and South's view of the dummy, South was not too optimistic about his chances. South was Larry Weiss of Los Angeles. However, after some thought his attitude brightened considerably as he realized two important factors:

First, the heart queen would likely fall doubleton in the East hand. West would certainly not have led from that card, and, further, it was improbable that he had led a singleton trump.

Second, West's opening bid clearly marked him with all the remaining high cards and West was a prime target to suffer an excruciating squeeze.

Dummy's top hearts were played, dropping the queen. The spade ace was cashed and a diamond was ruffed. The spade finesse was taken against the queen and the remaining spades were cashed, retaining the lead in dummy.

Another diamond ruff placed the lead in the South hand for the run of all the hearts. On the play of the last heart, West had no safe discards, since he either had to discard the diamond ace or to unguard his Q-J of clubs to establish declarer's 10 of clubs.

Seven hearts bid and made! West was not only sorry that he had opened the bidding; he was sorry to be alive.

SQUEEZE PLAY FOR GOLF GREAT
"Arnie Sinks His Opponents"

Arnold Palmer, our century's most electrifying golfer, can also introduce some high-voltage situations at the bridge table.

Witness Arnold's "come-from-behind charge" in today's hand, played in a recent rubber bridge game at Arnie's luxurious new Bay Hill Club and Lodge in Orlando, Fla:

North-South vulnerable
Dealer South

```
                     NORTH
                     ♠ Q
                     ♥ A Q J 9 8 3
                     ◆ Q J 8
                     ♣ Q 8 2
  WEST                                    EAST
  ♠ 8 5 3 2                               ♠ 9 7 4
  ♥ K 6 2                                 ♥ 10 5 4
  ◆ K 6 3 2                               ◆ 9 7 5
  ♣ 7 6                                   ♣ 10 5 4 3
                     SOUTH
                     ♠ A K J 10 6
                     ♥ 7
                     ◆ A 10 4
                     ♣ A K J 9
```

The bidding:

South	West	North	East
1 ♠	Pass	2 ♥	Pass
3 ♣	Pass	4 ♥	Pass
4 NT	Pass	5 ♦	Pass
7 NT	Pass	Pass	Pass

Opening lead: Seven of clubs.

Palmer sat South and opened one spade. His hand was just under the strength required for a demand bid of two spades. After North's response of two hearts, Palmer's rebid of three clubs described a very strong hand and was forcing to game.

When North jumped to four hearts, Palmer could restrain himself no longer and, after checking for aces, leaped all the way to seven no-trump. He needed an eagle to win, and he was not going to wait for the next hand! He noticed, however, a momentary pause before the player at his left passed after the seven no-trump bid.

West opened the seven of clubs, which Palmer won in his hand. Palmer could count five spade tricks and four club tricks. The two red aces brought the total to eleven. A finesse was available in both red suits.

However, since Palmer held only a singleton heart, he could take only one heart finesse. Unless the heart king were a doubleton, even a successful heart finesse would not suffice.

The diamond finesse offered the better chance for success, since the finesse could be repeated if East held the diamond king. But Arnie remembered the pause and decided West could well hold both missing kings.

Palmer decided against either finesse and played the black suits instead! He crossed to dummy's spade queen, cashed dummy's club queen and returned to his hand with a high club. All the black cards had been played. on the play of the last spade the position was:

81

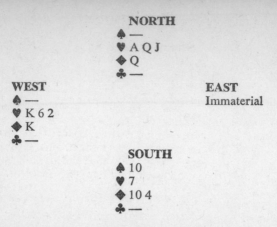

NORTH
♠ —
♥ A Q J
♦ Q
♣ —

WEST
♠ —
♥ K 6 2
♦ K
♣ —

EAST
Immaterial

SOUTH
♠ 10
♥ 7
♦ 10 4
♣ —

West could not discard safely. If West threw a heart, Palmer would discard dummy's diamond. A heart finesse would then provide three heart tricks and all thirteen tricks.

If West threw the diamond king, Palmer would discard dummy's diamond queen, cash the diamond 10 and then take the successful heart finesse for two heart tricks and all thirteen tricks.

Why did Palmer refuse both finesses in favor of the squeeze on West? West's pause gave him the clue. Obviously, he must have some of the same sensitive touch for bridge as he has for golf.

SLAM DOUBLE
"Leading Men in Trouble"

How would you like to compare your opening-lead judgment with that of Bobby Wolff and Omar Sharif?

This will be a pressure decision. A big swing to your team will be the result if you come up with the winning decision.

Today's hand was played in Dallas in the long bridge match played by The Aces against the Omar Sharif Bridge Circus.

Sitting West you hold:

♠ 8 7
♥ J 7 2
♦ 10 9 2
♣ K 9 8 6 5

What would you lead after this auction?

East	South	West	North
1 ♥	Dbl.	Pass	2 ♥
3 ♥	3 ♠	Pass	4 NT
Pass	5 ♣	Pass	6 ♠
Dbl.	Pass	Pass	Pass

Before you decide, an explanation of the bidding is necessary. East's one heart bid and South's double were normal. North's bid of two hearts was a standard cue bid, announcing an excellent hand and asking South to choose a suit. North's four no-trump was Blackwood, and South's response showed no ace.

Partner's double was the Lightner Slam Double, asking essentially, "Partner, do not lead my suit. I think we can beat this hand if you lead some other suit. Please figure out which one."

Both Wolff and Sharif reasoned that East's double was based on possession of a cashable ace and a void in one of the minor suits. What other holding could justify the double?

Okay, what minor suit do you lead? Wolff and Sharif both selected the club suit. It seemed reasonable to assume that partner was more likely to be void in clubs than in diamonds.

The entire hand was:

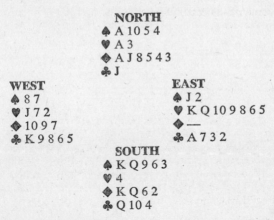

NORTH
♠ A 10 5 4
♥ A 3
♦ A J 8 5 4 3
♣ J

WEST
♠ 8 7
♥ J 7 2
♦ 10 9 7
♣ K 9 8 6 5

EAST
♠ J 2
♥ K Q 10 9 8 6 5
♦ —
♣ A 7 3 2

SOUTH
♠ K Q 9 6 3
♥ 4
♦ K Q 6 2
♣ Q 10 4

Did you join Wolff and Sharif in leading the club suit? Too bad—East was void in the shorter suit, diamonds. Unlucky for you, as it was for them. *Unless* you happened to lead the club king! If you did, surely after it held the trick, and with partner playing his deuce, you would shift to a diamond to beat the contract.

Both Sharif and Wolff had a doubled slam scored against them, and the net result was no swing. After East won the club ace, there was no return he could make and declarer had an easy time scoring his contract.

Score yourself as follows:

Diamond lead—Clairvoyant. Please don't ask us to play with you.

Low club lead—You're in excellent, but sorrowful, company.

Club king lead—Beautiful analysis. Takes care of all contingencies. Except, of course, when the club king would be the setting trick; if, for example, East were void in clubs and the opponents void in hearts.

COMBINING CHANCES
"If at First You Don't Succeed ... "

Sir Winston Churchill once said, "Men occasionally stumble over the truth, but most of them pick themselves up and hurry off as if nothing had happened."

Observe how Churchill's words apply to a slam hand played in a recent team-of-four match.

North-South vulnerable
Dealer South

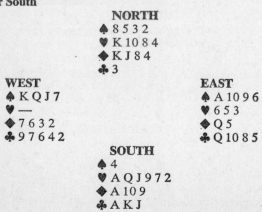

NORTH
- ♠ 8 5 3 2
- ♥ K 10 8 4
- ♦ K J 8 4
- ♣ 3

WEST
- ♠ K Q J 7
- ♥ —
- ♦ 7 6 3 2
- ♣ 9 7 6 4 2

EAST
- ♠ A 10 9 6
- ♥ 6 5 3
- ♦ Q 5
- ♣ Q 10 8 5

SOUTH
- ♠ 4
- ♥ A Q J 9 7 2
- ♦ A 10 9
- ♣ A K J

South	West	North	East
1 ♥	Pass	2 ♥	Pass
3 ♦	Pass	4 ♦	Pass
4 NT	Pass	5 ♣	Pass
6 ♥	Pass	Pass	Pass

Opening lead: King of spades.

Over North's raise to two hearts, South made a general forcing bid of three diamonds. North raised diamonds, showing an original heart raise of upper range and "something" in diamonds. South's Blackwood bid revealed that only one ace was missing and the good slam was bid.

At one table, after the opening lead of the spade king and spade continuation, South ruffed and played three rounds of trumps. Next he played the diamond ace and then finessed a diamond, losing to East's doubleton queen. Down one.

"Sorry partner," said declarer after the session. "I decided to play West for the diamond queen after he showed a void in hearts."

"Certainly reasonable," replied his partner, "but I was hoping you'd play for the queen to lie over the jack."

"I used to do that, but I read in the Encyclopedia of Bridge that there is not much to that theory. In any event, whatever validity it may have is primarily limited to rubber bridge."

At this point, the discussion was interrupted by the termination of play in the other room. When it was found that a large loss had been sustained on his hand, both players asked Ace Billy Eisenberg about the line of play he had chosen to make the hand.

Billy explained. After the ruff of the second spade, he saw that a successful finesse in either minor suit would bring the hand home. (If a club finesse succeeded, two of dummy's diamonds could be discarded, eliminating South's diamond loser.) Since either finesse was a 50 percent chance, Eisenberg chose to combine his plays in both minor suits to improve his chances.

First, he played the A-K of diamonds. If this play succeeded in dropping either a doubleton or singleton queen, no finesse need be taken. If this play failed, the even chance of a straight club finesse was still available. Clearly, Eisenberg's play was superior and his success was clearly deserved.

Both players thanked Billy for his explanation. As they left together, one was overheard saying, "Now about that play for the queen lying over the jack . . ."

EXECUTING AN END PLAY
"Care Reaps a Reward"

Why do some players recognize the correct play only after it is too late? Sometimes it's discovery of the location of the opponents' cards. Many times it's because a tempting and good line of play was easily apparent.

Chuck Burger, well-known bridge champion from Detroit, found a way to improve his chances on today's hand played in a recent team-of-four match.

All vulnerable
South Dealer

```
                        NORTH
                        ♠ A J 6
                        ♥ 8 4 3 2
                        ♦ A Q 3
                        ♣ K J 6
     WEST                                EAST
     ♠ 7 4 3                             ♠ 5
     ♥ A K 10                            ♥ Q J 9 7
     ♦ J 9 4                             ♦ K 8 7 6
     ♣ 10 8 7 4                          ♣ Q 9 5 2
                        SOUTH
                        ♠ K Q 10 9 8 2
                        ♥ 6 5
                        ♦ 10 5 2
                        ♣ A 3
```

The bidding:

South	West	North	East
2 ♠*	Pass	4 ♠	Pass
Pass	Pass		

*6-12 high-card points.
Opening lead: King of hearts.

The bidding was the same at both tables. South opened with a weak two bid and North jumped directly to game. South's bid described a hand with a good six-card suit capable of producing about six tricks with spades as trumps. North's

86

jump to game was based on the hope that his hand would provide the four additional tricks required for game.

In one room, the defense started with three rounds of hearts, East playing high-low to encourage, South ruffing the third round. Declarer extracted three rounds of trumps ending in his hand. A low diamond was led to dummy and the queen finessed.

East won the king and returned a diamond, dislodging dummy's ace. Declarer played the club ace, followed by a low club to dummy's jack. The finesse lost to East's queen and the contract was defeated two tricks, two hearts, two diamonds and one club. Declarer had lost both minor suit finesses. Had either been successful, he would have made his contract.

When the hand was played in the other room, Chuck also realized that he would make the hand if either of the minor suit finesses would succeed. However, Chuck also saw another play that would provide an extra chance to make the contract.

Instead of extracting three rounds of trumps ending in his hand, Chuck extracted three rounds of trumps ending in dummy. Now he led the last heart from dummy.

When East played the queen, Chuck let him hold the trick and discarded a diamond. East was now stuck with the lead and could not escape giving Chuck his tenth trick via a free finesse in either minor suit.

What if East had held only three hearts? Chuck would then ruff the fourth heart and fall back on the chance of succeeding in either one of the minor-suit finesses. It cost Chuck nothing to play hearts first. He gave himself a small additional chance and was rewarded accordingly.

What did Chuck do that many players do not? He took a little extra care in analysis before he played the hand instead of waiting until the hand was over.

TWO CHANCES BETTER THAN ONE
"33 and 43 Add Up to More than 50!"

Two midway barkers offer you a proposition. One gives you a 50 percent chance of winning a prize. The second barker offers two 35 percent chances. Assuming equal cost and prizes, which barkers gets your business?

Did you give your business to the second barker? Wise decision. Two chances of 35 percent are better than one of 50 percent.

While this principle may be obvious at the carnival, it sometimes remains obscure at the bridge table. Today's hand is an example of combining two individually inferior plays to increase overall chances for success.

North-South vulnerable
Dealer South

                    NORTH
                    ♠ A J 9 2
                    ♥ 9 2
                    ♦ A 3
                    ♣ A J 8 7 4
    WEST   EAST
    ♠ Q 7 6   ♠ K 10 5 4
    ♥ Q 6 5   ♥ 4 3
    ♦ 10 7 5   ♦ J 9 8 6 2
    ♣ Q 10 9 5   ♣ 6 2
                    SOUTH
                    ♠ 8 3
                    ♥ A K J 10 8 7
                    ♦ K Q 4
                    ♣ K 3

The bidding:
Goldman
                                Lawrence
South   **West**   **North**   **East**
1 ♥   Pass   2 ♣   Pass
3 ♥   Pass   3 ♠   Pass
3 NT   Pass   6 ♥   Pass
Pass   Pass

Opening lead: Six of spades.

Playing Aces' Standard, the auction was straightforward. Bobby Goldman's jump rebid showed a fine suit and 16-19 points. Mike Lawrence reasoned that possession of three aces should provide a good play for slam.

The opening lead was best for the defense. It removed an entry to dummy and limited Goldman's choice of actions because of the immediate spade loser if the opponents gained the lead.

Goldman's problems involved the play of two suits, clubs and hearts. In the heart suit, he had two choices: take a first-round finesse or play the A-K, hoping for the drop of the queen. The finesse at 50 percent is clearly a better chance.

In the club suit, although a finesse against the queen would be a 50 percent chance in isolated circumstances, the chances of an opponent's first- or second-round ruff reduce the chances to about 43 percent.

Goldman combined his plays in both suits. He won the spade ace in dummy and played the ace and king of hearts, hoping to drop the queen. When this failed, he played the club king and a low club to dummy's jack.

Then the losing spade was discarded on the ace of clubs. Bobby made his contract, losing only to the queen of trumps.

Bobby combined the second best play in the trump suit (approximately 33 percent) together with his play of the club suit (approximately 43 percent). Like the choice of two 35 percent chances being better than one 50 percent chance, Goldman chose the overall better line of play. Note that the contract would fail if the best individual play is taken (trump finesse).

Remember the following general rule: If success depends upon either one of two chances, your total chance is more than either one. If success depends upon both of two chances, your total chance is less than either one.

BIDDING INFLUENCES PLAY
"Silence Could Have Been Golden"

The bidding often guides an alert declarer to the winning line of play. Today's hand demonstrates this point twice. The hand was played in a major team championship, with both declarers drawing the correct inferences from two different bidding sequences.

All vulnerable
Dealer West

	NORTH	
	♠ J 7 5 2	
	♥ A 10 4	
	♦ A Q 6	
	♣ 9 4 3	
WEST		**EAST**
♠ 10 9		♠ Q 8 6 3
♥ J 9		♥ 7 3
♦ J 9 8		♦ K 7 5 4 3
♣ A K Q 8 7 5		♣ J 10
	SOUTH	
	♠ A K 4	
	♥ K Q 8 6 5 2	
	♦ 10 2	
	♣ 6 2	

The bidding:

West	Wolff North	East	Jacoby South
3 ♣	Pass	Pass	3 ♥
Pass	4 ♥	Pass	Pass
Pass			

Opening lead: King of clubs.

When played by Aces Jim Jacoby and Bobby Wolff, West opened the bidding with three clubs. East-West were playing that a minor suit preemptive three bid promised a solid six-card suit and no other prime cards. Jacoby, therefore, had good justification for finding the right line of play.

West opened the king of clubs and continued with the queen ace, Jacoby ruffing the third round. Jacoby correctly assumed that East had both the spade queen and diamond king. Trumps were drawn and the A-K of spades played.

Jacoby played off all of his remaining trumps and forced East to reduce to three cards. East was trapped. If he blanked his spade queen, a spade lead would force him to lead a diamond into dummy's A-Q. If he blanked the diamond king, Jacoby would be able to score both the ace and queen by reading the position and dropping East's king.

East made things as difficult as possible and blanked the diamond king. However, Jim played correctly and made his contract by playing the diamond ace and felling the king.

When the hand was replayed in the other room, the auction was different.

Lawrence		Hamman	
West	North	East	South
Pass	Pass	Pass	1 ♥
2 ♣	3 ♥	Pass	4 ♥
Pass	Pass	Pass	

With Aces Mike Lawrence and Bob Hamman holding the East-West cards, Lawrence passed the West hand, since a three-club bid in their partnership has a different meaning. However, after South opened the bidding, Mike overcalled two clubs, and this North-South pair also reached the heart game. Sitting South was Jeff Reubens of New York City. He played the hand in exactly the same fashion as did Jim Jacoby.

Jeff had available to him the same information that Jim had. Only in a different form. Three rounds of clubs revealed Mike's club holding. Mike's original pass precluded his holding any other prime cards, and Jeff followed the same course that Jim did to make his contract.

One might deduce that sometimes it is better not to bid at all because of the information that bidding may reveal to an alert declarer. Certainly there is much truth in this. But not on this hand.

Observe that even if neither of the two Wests bid, the normal play of three rounds of clubs will expose the situation to declarer. Today's West was destined for a loss before he picked up his cards.

PUTTING THE PRESSURE ON THE OPPONENTS
"Surprise! I Made It!"

Tommy Prothro, famous coach and tactician of UCLA's Bruins, can also display winning tactics at the bridge table. Witness his strategy in today's hand, played recently in a team-of-four match:

North-South vulnerable
Dealer South

                          NORTH
                          ♠ 5 4 2
                          ♥ 7 2
                          ♦ K 9 6 4 3
                          ♣ K Q 4

        WEST   **EAST**
        ♠ 9 6   ♠ K Q 10 8 7 3
        ♥ J 10 9 8 6   ♥ A K 4
        ♦ 8 7 5   ♦ Q J
        ♣ 10 8 6   ♣ 9 2

                          SOUTH
                          ♠ A J
                          ♥ Q 5 3
                          ♦ A 10 2
                          ♣ A J 7 5 3

The bidding:

South	West	North	East
1 NT	Pass	2 NT	3 ♠
3 NT	Pass	Pass	Pass

Opening lead: Nine of spades.

The bidding was the same at both tables. North raised to
two no-trump, holding eight high-card points and a five-card
suit. East refused to be shut out of the bidding and bid three
spades. (Note that East can hold his losses to down two at a
three-spade contract—a reasonable price to pay against a vulnerable game.)

South continued on to game on the strength of the long
club suit.

At the first table, the opening lead of the spade nine was
covered by East's queen, South winning the ace. Declarer had
seven more top tricks in clubs and diamonds. Prospects for
the ninth trick lay only in the diamond suit, since he could not
allow the opponents to gain the lead.

Declarer ran five club tricks to exert pressure on the defenders and in hopes of finding a clue concerning diamonds.
West discarded two hearts. East discarded a low heart and two
spades.

When South played his ace of diamonds followed by his 10
of diamonds, East dropping the jack under the ace, South had

a sheer guess concerning East's diamonds—singleton jack or Q-J doubleton.

South guessed wrong and finessed. East won his queen and took the rest of the tricks with his good spades and hearts.

When Prothro played the hand, he also won the first trick with the ace of spades. However, Tommy realized that even if he was lucky in finding a favorable diamond position, he would still be reduced to a guess at the critical moment. Therefore, Tommy decided to fall back on a favorite football tactic—surprise.

Tommy reasoned that he would not be able to surprise West by first running the clubs, thereby disclosing possession of eight tricks. Instead, he played the ace of diamonds at trick two, followed by the 10 of diamonds at trick three.

When West followed small, Tommy played East for the Q-J doubleton to make his contract. Tommy reasoned that if West held Q-8-7-5 or J-8-7-5 of diamonds, he would have undoubtedly covered the 10 of diamonds with his honor to prevent declarer from taking five diamond tricks. When West failed to cover, East was "marked" with the other honor.

Surprise is not only a winning tactic at football; it also has its place at the bridge table.

CHOICE IN THE PLAY
"Best Laid Plans of Mice and Lawrence"

Mike Lawrence of The Aces earned a star award for his play of today's hand. The hand was played in an early round of the Spingold Tournament.

Study only the bidding, the lead and the North-South hands (place your thumbs over the East-West hands). Then develop a plan of play and compare it with Mike's to see if you would have also earned an award.

West opens the spade 4, the queen is played from dummy, East plays the 6. Plan your play.

All vulnerable
Dealer East

NORTH
♠ Q 10
♥ A Q J 4
♦ K J 10 6
♣ J 7 5

WEST
♠ A K 5 4
♥ 10 5
♦ 7 3 2
♣ K 6 4 3

EAST
♠ 9 6 3 2
♥ K 8 7 3 2
♦ 9 8
♣ Q 2

SOUTH
♠ J 8 7
♥ 9 6
♦ A Q 5 4
♣ A 10 9 8

The bidding:

Hamman North	East	Lawrence South	West
	Pass	Pass	Pass
1 ♥	Pass	2 NT	Pass
3 NT	Pass	Pass	Pass

Opening lead: Four of spades.

The winning play is to refuse the heart finesse. If the heart finesse is taken, East wins and the hand is defeated because declarer can take only eight tricks (one spade, four diamonds, one club and only two hearts) before the defense takes five (three spades, one heart and one club).

Mike reasoned: Obviously West underled the A-K of spades. If West led from a five-card suit, the hand could not be made unless West also had the heart king (one spade, three hearts, four diamonds and one club). However, if West had five spades and the heart king, why had he not opened the bidding after two passes?

If West had only four spades and the heart king, then all plays would win. (West could not have both club honors because of his failure to open the bidding.)

Mike concluded that his best chance for success required an even division of the spade suit and either or both club honors in the East hand. Aside from the inferences drawn from the bidding, the probability of developing three club tricks

94

was better than developing three heart tricks.

Mike's reasoning guided him to the winning line of play. He rejected the enticing heart finesse and instead chose the double club finesse. He won the spade queen in dummy and played the club jack, allowing it to ride to West's king.

East-West could now take three more spade tricks, but Lawrence made his contract. He took one spade, one heart, four diamonds, and three clubs. (The fall of the club queen made the repeated finesse unnecessary.)

Mike applied several basic principles. He analyzed all available information deduced from the bidding. He counted his tricks and selected the plan most likely to succeed that was consistent with the bidding.

DUPLICATE VS. RUBBER BRIDGE
"Pessimism Triumphs over Optimism"

*"Two men look out through the same bars.
One sees the mud and one the stars."*

Frederick Langbridge's quotation applies quite often to the game of bridge. This is especially apparent when the same hand is played more than once and several players are confronted with an identical problem.

Today's hand was played in a recent tournament. Witness the vast difference in approach by he who sees mud and he who sees the stars:

All vulnerable
Dealer North

```
                    NORTH
                    ♠ A J 4
                    ♥ 10
                    ♦ Q 10 9 8 7 3
                    ♣ A 9 2
   WEST                                 EAST
   ♠ 9 7 6                              ♠ K 10
   ♥ K 8 5 4                            ♥ Q J 7 3 2
   ♦ K 6 5 4                            ♦ 2
   ♣ K Q                                ♣ 8 6 5 4 3
                    SOUTH
                    ♠ Q 8 5 3 2
                    ♥ A 9 6
                    ♦ A J
                    ♣ J 10 7
```

The bidding:

North	East	South	West
1 ♦	Pass	1 ♠	Pass
2 ♠	Pass	4 ♠	Pass
Pass	Pass		

Opening lead: King of clubs.

At duplicate scoring, the declarer is obligated to become an optimist. (He must attempt to take as many tricks as the most favorable distribution of the cards might make possible.) The club ace was won in dummy and a diamond led and finessed, West winning the king.

West returned the diamond 4, which East ruffed with the spade 10. A club was led to West's queen and another diamond led. East ruffed with his spade king, South discarding a club. East led the third round of clubs and South was in trouble.

Regardless of what he did, West could not be prevented from making a trump trick. If South ruffed low, West would overruff. If South ruffed with the queen, West would eventually make a trump trick by covering any trump led by South. Down two.

The pessimist played for both kings to be off-side and chose a cautious road. He won the opening lead with the club ace, and played the spade 4 from dummy, East winning the king.

East shifted to a heart (best) and declarer won the ace. A low spade was played to dummy's ace followed by the ace and jack of diamonds. (Losing a diamond finesse would be fatal since West could return the last trump while declarer's ace blocked the diamond suit.)

West won the diamond king and continued hearts. Declarer ruffed in dummy and discarded his last heart on the diamond queen. A diamond was ruffed to enter his hand to remove West's last trump. A club trick was conceded and South made his contract, losing one spade, one diamond and one club.

Who played correctly, the optimist or the pessimist?

In duplicate pairs, the optimist played "correctly" but lost the hand. Successful duplicate players play for overtricks and rarely can afford pessimism. However, in rubber and international match points bridge, a pessimistic view towards overtricks is best and safety of the contract should receive top priority.

"Going Down at Trick No. 1"

Among some top players, one rarely mentions or hears of an error. Instead, one learns to refer to such things as "a wrong view," "a judgment situation," etc. Even in the most flagrant cases, ego protection remains paramount.

The star player caught with egg on his face says protectively, "I backed my judgment and it turned out badly." With this statement he translates a bonehead error into an act of heroism and readies himself for the next battle.

Witness how today's declarer "backed his judgment" in the play of today's hand. For obvious reasons, today's South shall remain unnamed.

North-South vulnerable
Dealer South

<pre>
                    NORTH
                    ♠ J 10 8 7 2
                    ♥ K 3
                    ♦ A Q 10 3
                    ♣ A 2
    WEST   EAST
    ♠ 6 4   ♠ 5
    ♥ J 10 9 7 5   ♥ A Q 6 2
    ♦ 9 5 2   ♦ K J 7
    ♣ Q 10 4   ♣ J 9 8 6 3
                    SOUTH
                    ♠ A K Q 9 3
                    ♥ 8 4
                    ♦ 8 6 4
                    ♣ K 7 5
</pre>

The bidding:

South	West	North	East
1 ♠	Pass	4 ♣ *	Pass
4 ♠	Pass	Pass	Pass

*Swiss bid.
Opening lead: Jack of hearts.

North's jump to four clubs was a Swiss bid showing a balanced hand, four or more trumps and 15-16 support points. South signed off at four spades, which became the final contract.

West opened the jack of hearts, covered with dummy's king, East winning the ace. A low heart was led to West's 9, and West shifted to the diamond 9.

South finessed the 10 and East won the jack. East exited with a trump. Declarer won, drew another trump, and had no choice but to attempt another diamond finesse. This failed and the contract was defeated one trick.

In the postmortem, South was asked, "How come you didn't make the hand?" The question alerted South to the fact that he may have made an error. "I backed my judgment," he claimed while quickly searching for the flaw in his play. Can you see where South went wrong?

South should not have played dummy's heart king at the first trick. After the duck, it does West no good to continue hearts, so he shifts to diamonds. Declarer plays the ace and draws trumps.

Next, the two high clubs are played and declarer's third club ruffed. The king of hearts places East on lead and forces him to concede a ruff and sluff or lead from his king of diamonds. Either way South makes his contract.

(If hearts are continued at trick two, declarer eliminates clubs from his hand and dummy and finesses the 10 of diamonds, placing East in the same predicament.)

South was now ready with his defense. "I played West for the ace of hearts," he said. "You mean you played him for an underlead of the ace of hearts?" his inquisitors continued. "Well, his table manner made me very suspicious and I was willing to back my judgment."

This served as a transition to another subject. However, no one was convinced. How about you?

DESCHAPELLES COUP
"Sacrificing One's Honor"

The Merrimac Coup is a fascinating play that involves the deliberate sacrifice of a high card with the object of knocking out a vital entry in an opponent's hand.

Today's hand is an example of the Deschappeles Coup. It is similar to the Merrimac Coup in that a deliberate sacrifice of a high card is made. However, its object is to establish an entry to partner's hand.

All vulnerable
Dealer North

                        NORTH
                        ♠ 7 6 2
                        ♥ A 3
                        ♦ A J 2
                        ♣ A J 10 8 4

WEST   **EAST**
♠ Q 10 9 8 4 3   ♠ K 5
♥ Q 7 6 5   ♥ K 8 4 2
♦ 7 6   ♦ 8 5 4 3
♣ 2   ♣ K Q 6

                        SOUTH
                        ♠ A J
                        ♥ J 10 9
                        ♦ K Q 10 9
                        ♣ 9 7 5 3

The bidding:

			Wolff
North	**East**	**South**	**West**
1 ♣	Pass	1 ♦	Pass
2 ♦	Pass	2 NT	Pass
3 NT	Pass	Pass	Pass

Opening lead: Ten of spades.

The bidding was routine. North raised diamonds in preference to rebidding clubs. South's 11 high-card points and good
intermediates justified his invitational bid of two no-trump
and North bid on to game.

West led the 10 of spades, East played the king and South
ducked, hoping to sever communication in the spade suit.
South succeeded in isolating West's spade suit, but his problems were far from over.

Declarer could count two major suit aces and four diamond
tricks. He needed three club tricks to make his contract. He
planned on two finesses into the East hand, hoping to keep
West from gaining the lead. At trick three, declarer finessed a
club into the East hand.

Today's East was Walter C. Wolff Jr. of San Antonio,
brother of Ace Bobby Wolff. Walter won his queen and made
the only play to defeat the hand. The heart king! The Deschapelles Coup.

Declarer could win or refuse the trick to no avail. If declarer ducked, Walter would continue and then, when on lead with the club king, would lead another heart to West's queen. An entry was created to the established spade suit.

Note that any return other than the heart king by Walter would enable South to make the hand. West would be unable to gain the lead to run the spades before South could take sufficient tricks to make his contract (one spade, one heart, four diamonds and three clubs).

Like the Merrimac Coup, the Deschapelles Coup is an unusual and exciting play. Sometimes even amusing. Especially when declarer turns up with the missing honors.

However, for a defender, one successful coup is well worth many futile attempts.

GUESSING THE PLAY
"Coin Toss Came up 'Aces' "

Swing hands determine the results of bridge matches—be they for the world championship or for first prize at an afternoon tea. A swing is the difference between the actual score made and "what might have been" were the bidding, play, or defense different.

In team bridge matches, the swing is emphasized because the identical hand is played twice for a direct comparison of results achieved by both teams.

Most major swings are produced by different bidding systems or styles, different opening leads, differences in defense or declarer play, and even whether it is North or South who becomes declarer at the same contract.

Rarely is a swing produced when the bidding and the play to the first five tricks is identical at both tables. Today's hand is one of those rare exceptions.

All vulnerable
Dealer South

                        NORTH
                        ♠ Q 9 7 3
                        ♥ J 9 3
                        ◆ A 8 7 5 3
                        ♣ A

    WEST   **EAST**
    ♠ K 6   ♠ A J 8 5 4
    ♥ A 5   ♥ 10 8
    ◆ Q J 6 4   ◆ 9 2
    ♣ J 10 9 7 5   ♣ 8 4 3 2

                        SOUTH
                        ♠ 10 2
                        ♥ K Q 7 6 4 2
                        ◆ K 10
                        ♣ K Q 6

The bidding:

South	West	North	East
1 ♥	Pass	2 ◆	Pass
2 ♥	Pass	4 ♥	Pass
Pass	Pass		

Opening lead: Jack of clubs.

This hand was played by The Aces and the Omar Sharif Bridge Circus. The bidding was identical in both rooms.

Both declarers won the opening lead with the club ace and started trumps, the play going 3, 8, queen and ace. Both Wests found the only defense to give the declarer a problem. King and another spade! Both Easts won the spade ace and led back a small spade.

Both declarers studied long and hard. We know the heart distribution; they did not. Claude Delmouly for the Circus and Bobby Goldman for The Aces were both trying to determine: (1) Had West really started with only two spades? (2) Who had the heart 10?

If West had only two spades and the heart 10, declarer must ruff with the trump king to prevent West from ruffing with his 10 and scoring the setting trick.

Both declarers ruffed with the heart king! When both declarers led a low heart, West playing the 5, it was time for another long study.

Delmouly played for West to have an original trump holding of A-10-5 and finessed dummy's 9. This lost to East's 10 and Delmouly was down. Goldman played for the actual distribution and made his contract.

Why did one player play for the finesse and the other for the drop? Who knows? The play is a toss-up.

Identification and classification of the thoughts that race through a player's mind during these periods of high stress would tax a computer! Players who are in top form "guess" these solutions; players who are not in top form do not.

The Aces gained 720 points or 12 international match points on this deal. A large swing that depended upon a decision concerning a 10-spot!

TIMING IN DECLARER'S PLAY
"Ace's Wife One Up on Aces"

It gets downright embarrassing when the wife of one of The Aces has to tell some of the fellows how a hand should have been played! But it happened in Stockholm in the world pair's championship with 158 tables in play.

This is the deal that caused ever-so-many red faces.

East-West vulnerable
Dealer East

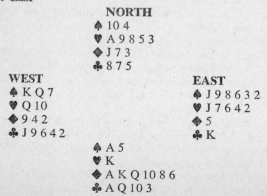

```
                    NORTH
                    ♠ 10 4
                    ♥ A 9 8 5 3
                    ♦ J 7 3
                    ♣ 8 7 5
    WEST                              EAST
    ♠ K Q 7                          ♠ J 9 8 6 3 2
    ♥ Q 10                           ♥ J 7 6 4 2
    ♦ 9 4 2                          ♦ 5
    ♣ J 9 6 4 2                      ♣ K
                    SOUTH
                    ♠ A 5
                    ♥ K
                    ♦ A K Q 10 8 6
                    ♣ A Q 10 3
```

The bidding:

East	South	West	North
Pass	1 ◆	Pass	1 ♥
Pass	3 ♣	Pass	3 ◆
Pass	4 NT	Pass	5 ◆
Pass	6 ◆	Pass	Pass
Pass			

Opening lead: King of spades.

South was close to an opening demand bid but chose the conservative course. However, after hearing about a little diamond support from North, nothing could stop him from contracting for slam.

Declarer had his work cut out for him at six diamonds. He knew that most pairs would be in three no-trump with the North-South cards and that, unless he made his contract, he was going to receive a very poor score.

Declarer won the spade ace and cashed his king of hearts. Dummy was entered with the jack of diamonds and his losing spade was discarded on dummy's ace of hearts. Next declarer led a club, and, when East obligingly played the king, declarer captured it with his ace. Can you blame him?

Consider his problem after winning the club ace. He must arrange to trump one of his losing clubs in dummy, which is not as easy as it appears.

If trumps divide evenly, there is no problem. Declarer can play a second trump and then play queen and another club. Later he can trump his fourth club with dummy's trump.

However, if he plays a second trump and trumps do not divide evenly—and he won't know until he plays the suit—then, if the player who wins the third round of clubs has a trump left, he will lead it and prevent declarer from ruffing his fourth club. This line of play will result in defeat.

As the cards lie, declarer can play the queen of clubs and another club to make the hand. But suppose East had started with two diamonds and only one club? East would ruff the club queen and declarer would lose two club tricks and his slam.

How can South tell which is the better play? Take the second round of trumps or play the queen and another club?

Barbara Hamman, wife of Ace Bob Hamman, was listening to the postmortem discussion.

"Why not," she asked, "duck the king of clubs?" South can ruff whatever East returns with a high trump and play a second round of trumps to find out if they divide evenly. If so, there is no problem; South ruffs his low club in dummy.

If not, South can play his A-Q of clubs and ruff his last club with dummy's small trump. He still has two high trumps in his hand, one to ruff dummy's exit high; the other to extract West's 9 of trumps.

Barbara's line of play makes it unnecessary to guess whether trumps were two-two or three-one. You wouldn't believe how many red faces there were!

SECOND HAND HIGH
"Rising to the Occasion"

The key to success in almost any endeavor is timing. Contract bridge is no exception. Countless examples exist where the wrong play at the right time is successful; the right play at the wrong time is not.

Today's hand was played in a team contest. It illustrates the importance of timing for the defense.

North-South vulnerable
Dealer South

                    NORTH
                    ♠ 10 8 6 2
                    ♥ J 10 5 4
                    ♦ A Q 10 2
                    ♣ 5

WEST   EAST
♠ J 7 4 3   ♠ A 5
♥ A 6   ♥ K 7 3 2
♦ 9 7 6   ♦ 8 5 4
♣ Q 7 3 2   ♣ K 8 6 4

                    SOUTH
                    ♠ K Q 9
                    ♥ Q 9 8
                    ♦ K J 3
                    ♣ A J 10 9

The bidding:

South	West	North	East
1 NT	Pass	2 ♣*	Pass
2 ♦	Pass	2 NT	Pass
3 NT	Pass	Pass	Pass

*Stayman Convention.
Opening lead: Three of spades.

After South's standard opening of one no-trump, North used the Stayman Convention in an effort to locate an eight-card major suit fit. When South denied a four-card major suit, North retreated to two no-trump. South's good intermediates convinced him to bid the vulnerable game.

West's opening spade lead was won by East's ace, and the spade 5 was returned, South winning the queen. South led the diamond 3 to dummy's 10 and played a low heart from dummy, East and declarer playing low. West won the heart ace, played a third spade and established his jack.

South knocked out East's heart king, won East's return and claimed his contract. He took two spades, two hearts, four diamonds and one club.

When the hand was replayed in the other room, Edgar Kaplan, famed player, coach and author (*Bridge World* magazine), was in the East chair. Edgar was also defending three no-trump, reached via the same bidding sequence.

The play to the first three tricks was identical. However, when declarer played a low heart from dummy at trick four, Edgar rose with his king! Heresy? Second hand low? What was Edgar up to?

Edgar won the heart king and shifted to a low club. Declarer was helpless.

If he took his ace, the defense would collect two clubs, two hearts and one spade. If he finessed, West would win his queen and shift back to spades to clear that suit. The heart ace would provide entry to cash the spade jack and would give the defense two spades, two hearts and one club.

Note that the play of the heart king is the only successful line of defense. A club lead by West will not succeed because declarer will then be able to capture East's king and return the suit, taking, in all, two spades, four diamonds and three clubs.

Perfect timing by Edgar Kaplan. He alertly analyzed the situation and made it possible for the defense to play each suit in the correct sequence. Second hand low is usually correct but not when it is right for second hand to be on lead.

BRILLIANT DEFENSIVE DUCK
"Seeing Is Believing"

Everyone has at some time or other mistakenly played the wrong card—usually for a bad score.

Sometimes luck provides a second chance, but only if you act as if nothing happened. One gasp, or a futile attempt to grab the card before it hits the table, will give the show away and kill any hope of a second chance.

Observe West's defense of today's game hand which illustrates this point.

Both vulnerable
Dealer South

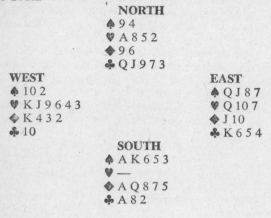

NORTH
♠ 9 4
♥ A 8 5 2
♦ 9 6
♣ Q J 9 7 3

WEST
♠ 10 2
♥ K J 9 6 4 3
♦ K 4 3 2
♣ 10

EAST
♠ Q J 8 7
♥ Q 10 7
♦ J 10
♣ K 6 5 4

SOUTH
♠ A K 6 5 3
♥ —
♦ A Q 8 7 5
♣ A 8 2

The bidding:

South	West	North	East
1 ♠	Pass	1 NT	Pass
3 ♦	Pass	3 ♠	Pass
4 ♠	Pass	Pass	Pass

Opening lead: Ten of clubs.

Over North's one no-trump response (6-9 points) South forced with three diamonds to find the best game contract. North showed a preference for South's first suit and South bid the spade game.

Sitting West was Ace Billy Eisenberg. His opening lead of the club 10 was covered with dummy's jack, which won the trick when East refused to cover. A small diamond was led from dummy, East followed with the 10, and declarer played the queen.

Eisenberg followed with the deuce! Had he pulled the wrong card?

Examine the play if Billy wins declarer's queen with his king. Since a spade or diamond return is hopeless, a heart is returned at trick three. Dummy wins the ace and discards his losing club. Next, declarer plays the 9 of diamonds to the ace, intending to establish the suit via a ruff.

However, the fall of East's jack establishes the suit without a ruff and declarer can start trumps, conceding two trump tricks to East. Declarer makes his contract, losing two spades and a diamond.

Back to the actual play. After Billy's duck of the diamond queen, declarer quite naturally placed the diamond king with East. Therefore, declarer played the ace of diamonds and ruffed a third diamond with dummy's 4 of trumps.

East overruffed with his 7 and returned a club. Billy ruffed with his spade deuce and returned the king of diamonds. East overruffed dummy once again and led another club, Billy ruffing with his spade 10. Down one.

Had Eisenberg ducked intentionally or had he pulled the wrong card? If he had pulled the wrong card, he gave no sign. If he had, declarer would have had no problem with the hand.

P. S. Billy received a star award for the defense of today's hand.

CREATING AN ENTRANCE
"ALAKAZAN! AN ENTRY"

Lainie Kazan, celebrated singer and TV personality, recently visited Dallas, home of The Aces, for a singing engagement at the Fairmont Hotel. During her stay, a couple of our bachelor Aces managed to arrange a friendly bridge match.

Lainie maintained that she really didn't know too much about bridge. But, being a good sport, she consented to play a short team match.

Observe Lainie's play of today's game contract. Lainie sat South and I sat North.

North-South vulnerable
Dealer South

                    NORTH
                    ♠ 9 8 3
                    ♥ 7 2
                    ♦ A J 9 8 5 3
                    ♣ J 5
    WEST   EAST
    ♠ K J 7 6   ♠ Q 5 2
    ♥ 10 6 4   ♥ J 5
    ♦ Q 6 4   ♦ K 10 7 2
    ♣ 9 7 4   ♣ K 10 8 3
                    SOUTH
                    ♠ A 10 4
                    ♥ A K Q 9 8 3
                    ♦ —
                    ♣ A Q 6 2

The bidding:
    Lainie   Corn
    South   West   North   East
    1 ♥   Pass   1 NT   Pass
    3 ♣   Pass   3 ♥   Pass
    4 ♥   Pass   Pass   Pass

Opening lead: Four of hearts.

Lainie bid the hand well. She opened in her long suit and, over my one no-trump response, she jump shifted to three clubs. Over my simple preference bid of three hearts, she settled for a game contract and bid four hearts. The same contract was reached in both rooms.

When the hand was played the first time, declarer won the trump lead in his hand, covering East's jack with his queen. Declarer could count nine tricks—six hearts, one spade and two clubs. A tenth trick was the diamond ace. All that was needed was an entry to dummy to cash the ace of diamonds.

Declarer drew two more rounds of trumps and then led a low club to dummy's jack. If West had the club king, an even chance, declarer could reach dummy with the club jack to cash the ace of diamonds.

Unfortunately, East won the club jack with his king and returned a spade. Declarer could no longer make the hand and had to concede two clubs and two spades to the defense. Down one.

When Lainie was the declarer, she also won East's heart jack with her queen. But what did she play at trick two? The queen of clubs!

Observe how this neutralized the defense. If East took the queen with the king, the club jack would provide entry to dummy's diamond ace. If East refused to take the king, Lainie would play the ace and another club, ruffing with dummy's trump 7.

In actual play, East won the king of clubs, hoping that West held the ace. Lainie won the spade return, crossed to dummy's club jack, cashed the diamond ace and discarded a low spade. A diamond was ruffed, trumps drawn, and ten tricks claimed.

Well played by Lainie. She found the only way to force an entry to the North hand to cash the diamond ace. She obviously knows more about bridge than she claims.

CLEVER DEFENSE
"Wheels within Wheels"

Mike Ledeen, professor of history at Washington University of St. Louis, reports today's interesting hand. It is an exciting example of inference and counterinference between the defense and the declarer.

North-South vulnerable
Dealer South

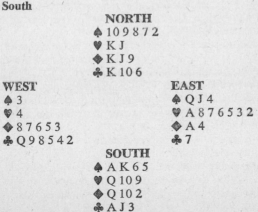

```
                        NORTH
                        ♠ 10 9 8 7 2
                        ♥ K J
                        ♦ K J 9
                        ♣ K 10 6
        WEST                            EAST
        ♠ 3                             ♠ Q J 4
        ♥ 4                             ♥ A 8 7 6 5 3 2
        ♦ 8 7 6 5 3                     ♦ A 4
        ♣ Q 9 8 5 4 2                   ♣ 7
                        SOUTH
                        ♠ A K 6 5
                        ♥ Q 10 9
                        ♦ Q 10 2
                        ♣ A J 3
```

The bidding:

South	West	North	East
1 NT	Pass	2 ♣*	2 ♥
2 ♠	Pass	4 ♠	Pass
Pass	Pass		

*Stayman convention.
Opening lead: Four of hearts.

South opened a standard 16-18 point one no-trump and North bid two clubs in an attempt to find a spade fit. Over East's overcall, South showed his four-card major suit, which North raised to game.

West opened his singleton heart, which East won with his ace. Before East played to the second trick, he took time for study. He reasoned that West could have only a singleton spade, since South's bid of two spades showed a four-card suit. East was also sure that West's lead of the heart 4 was a singleton.

East looked ahead and visualized the course of the defense if, at trick two, he returned the heart 8 (suit preference signal). West would ruff and return a diamond to East's ace. Another heart lead would be futile, since West had no more trumps.

Worse, East would not be able to hide this fact from declarer! If he returned a heart, West's failure to ruff with an honor would reveal the spade position. On the other hand, if East didn't return a heart, South would surely be able to draw the correct inference.

East resolved his dilemma by cashing the diamond ace at trick two and then allowing West to ruff the heart. When West exited with a diamond, declarer fully expected East to ruff. He was quite relieved when East followed suit.

However, his relief was short-lived. Declarer played a high spade and eventually lost a spade trick to East for down one. East was congratulated for his fine defense.

Ledeen points out, however, that while East did well to cloud the issue, declarer should have drawn the correct inferences anyway. If East had not held the Q-J-4 of spades, why would he first cash the diamond ace?

It would have been a simple matter for East to save the ace as an entry for an overruff position in hearts. The fact that East played as he did should have alerted South to the winning line of play in spades—the double finesse.

A clear and simple case of "I knew that he knew because he knew that I knew."

REFUSING TO OVERRUFF
"Hams That Hog the Spotlight"

Who has never played against a bidding hog?

One of the game's super irritants, he always manages to bid one more, creating havoc wherever he can. His overbearing aggressiveness sometimes ends in disaster, but not often enough to compensate for the exasperation he spreads.

Observe how a bidding hog was repaid in the defense of today's slam hand.

Both vulnerable
Dealer East

```
                    NORTH
                  ♠ A 7 6 5
                  ♥ 6 4
                  ◆ Q 9 7
                  ♣ K Q J 3
     WEST                          EAST
   ♠ K 3 2                       ♠ —
   ♥ A K 10 9 8 7                ♥ Q J 3
   ◆ A 2                         ◆ K J 8 6 4 3
   ♣ 6 4                         ♣ A 7 5 2
                    SOUTH
                  ♠ Q J 10 9 8 4
                  ♥ 5 2
                  ◆ 10 5
                  ♣ 10 9 8
```

The bidding:

North	East	South	West
	1 ◆	Pass	1 ♥
Dbl.	2 ♥	2 ♠	4 NT
Pass	5 ◆	Pass	6 ♥
Pass	Pass	6 ♠	Dbl.
Pass	Pass	Pass	

Note how the mere presence of the bidding hog affects a player's judgment. West, in an effort to close South's mouth, impulsively bid four no-trump.

Use of the Blackwood convention when holding a worthless doubleton is not a good policy. However, East-West reached a fine slam which would have been fulfilled except for the inevitable bid of six spades by South. West doubled in resignation.

West's opening lead of the heart king held the first trick.

He switched to the ace and another diamond, East signaling with the diamond eight. East won the second diamond with his jack, cashed the heart queen and continued with the diamond king.

South ruffed with one of his high trumps, and West cleverly discarded a club instead of overruffing. South was now able to capture West's trump king via a finesse. However, West's gambit convinced him that East had the spade king. Wouldn't you think so?

South played the queen of spades, and when West played low, South refused the spade finesse. Instead, he played dummy's spade ace, hoping to catch a singleton king. South was shocked when East discarded on the spade ace, and he realized what West had perpetrated.

South continued with another spade, West won his king and led his now lone club to East's ace. East returned a club for West to ruff. Down six—1,700 points.

Note that if West had merely overruffed with the spade king, the penalty would have been 300 points less. The penalty of 1,400 points would have been roughly equal to the value of the slam—1,430 points. A virtual standoff.

Which do you think West enjoyed more? Three hundred extra points or the satisfaction of getting even with South?

ACCEPTING OR REFUSING TRICK NO. 1
"Before You Grab the First One—Think, Think, Think!"

For the first time in 14 years, Italy was not one of the competing teams in the 1971 World Championship. The 1971 championship was scheduled in early May and was played in Taipei, Taiwan.

The previous year The Aces replaced Italy as world champions and defended their title in May. Five other teams participated. They represented South America (Brazil), the Far East (Taiwan), Europe (France), Australia, and North America (United States).

Roger Trezel and Pierre Jais were one of the pairs on the French team. They are an outstanding partnership and have had previous experience in world championship play.

Observe Trezel in action in the play of this hand. Trezel was South.

112

North-South vulnerable
Dealer South

                        NORTH
                        ♠ K 10 8 4
                        ♥ K 9 8 7 6
                        ♦ A 2
                        ♣ 4 3

WEST   **EAST**
♠ 6   ♠ 3 2
♥ 4 3   ♥ Q J 5
♦ K Q J 9 8 7 6   ♦ 10 5 4
♣ A Q J   ♣ 10 9 8 5 2

                        SOUTH
                        ♠ A Q J 9 7 5
                        ♥ A 10 2
                        ♦ 3
                        ♣ K 7 6

The bidding:

South	West	North	East
1 ♠	2 ♦	3 ♠	Pass
4 ♣	5 ♦	Pass	Pass
5 ♣	Pass	Pass	Pass

Opening lead: King of diamonds.

Against Trezel's five-spade contract, West selected the obvious lead of the diamond king. How was Trezel going to avoid the loss of one heart trick and two club tricks?

He played dummy's deuce of diamonds at the first trick! The defense was now helpless. Trezel won the diamond continuation with dummy's ace and discarded a heart from his hand.

Two rounds of trumps were played, followed by two high hearts and a heart ruff to establish the suit. Two of Trezel's clubs were discarded on dummy's hearts and the contract was made, declarer losing only one diamond and one club.

Note that the "automatic" play of dummy's diamond ace at trick one will condemn the hand to defeat. Declarer would not be able to prevent East from gaining the lead in the heart suit for the killing shift through declarer's king of clubs.

Another point of interest is that if West had been clairvoyant and had led a low diamond instead of the king, Trezel's opportunity for his imaginative play would have been thwarted. If declarer ducked, then East's diamond 10 would win the trick for the club shift. If declarer played the diamond ace, East would later gain entry in hearts for the same club shift.

DECEPTIVE PLAY
"Don't Trust the Announcer"

Charley Jones, television and radio sportscaster, can also give some play-by-play analyses to situations at the bridge table.

Witness Charley's inspired defense of today's hand played in a recent rubber bridge game in his home in La Jolla, California:

East-West vulnerable
Dealer East

```
                    NORTH
                    ♠ 8 7 2
                    ♥ A 10 3
                    ◆ A K Q 7
                    ♣ 10 8 4
   WEST                              EAST
   ♠ K J                            ♠ 10 4
   ♥ K Q J 8 7 5                    ♥ 9 4 2
   ◆ J 10 4 2                       ◆ 8 6 5
   ♣ 3                              ♣ A K 9 7 5
                    SOUTH
                    ♠ A Q 9 6 5 3
                    ♥ 6
                    ◆ 9 3
                    ♣ Q J 6 2
```

The bidding:

		Jones	
East	South	West	North
Pass	Pass	1 ♥	Pass
2 ♥	2 ♠	Pass	4 ♠
Pass	Pass	Pass	

Opening lead: Three of clubs.

After two passes, Jones opened the West hand with one heart. North's pass was proper in spite of his 13 high-card points. He had no convenient descriptive bid available.

An overcall in a four-card suit at the two level was unthink-

114

able and a takeout double was unattractive because of the flat distribution and the limited holding in spades. East raised to two hearts, and South, after having passed originally, interrupted with two spades. North lost no time in raising to game.

Jones didn't like his chances for taking too many heart tricks after partner's raise and therefore chose his singleton club as the opening lead. East won with king, and followed with the ace and a third round of clubs. Jones ruffed with the king of trumps. Had Jones dubbed one or had he pulled the wrong card?

Neither. Jones knew he needed a touchdown to win and he was going for it. He reasoned that declarer would undoubtedly play him for the king of trumps, since Jones had opened the bidding and since East had already shown the ace and king of clubs.

Therefore, Jones reasoned, if he ruffed with the jack, there would be no chance for him to score a trick with the king. Declarer, knowing the location of the king and having noted Jones' ruff with the jack, would undoubtedly snare Jones' king by refusing a finesse.

But what if Jones had started with a singleton king? To succeed, declarer now had to finesse twice through East's "obvious" holding of J-10-4.

Declarer decided to play Jones for a singleton king of spades, and Charley scored his jack of spades for the setting trick. If an equivalent play had been made on the football field while Charley Jones was at the microphone, he undoubtedly would have shown the play over and over via videotape instant replay.

FALSE CARDING
"Dishonesty Can Be the Best Policy"

Bud Dietrich, famous magician, entertainer and master of ceremonies, sometimes performs feats of magic at the bridge table. Playing a hand against Bud's defense is always exciting, since one never knows when a rabbit may pop out of the hat.

Observe how Bud played the ancient shell game on today's unfortunate declarer. Bud held today's East cards.

Both vulnerable
Dealer South

                          NORTH
                          ♠ J 8 7
                          ♥ A Q 6
                          ◆ 10 4 2
                          ♣ J 9 5 2

     WEST   EAST
     ♠ 6 5   ♠ A 2
     ♥ J 10 9 7 4   ♥ K 8 5 3 2
     ◆ 7 6 3   ◆ Q 8 5
     ♣ 8 7 4   ♣ Q 10 6

                          SOUTH
                          ♠ K Q 10 9 4 3
                          ♥ —
                          ◆ A K J 9
                          ♣ A K 3

The bidding:

South	West	North	East
2 ♠	Pass	3 ♠	Pass
6 ♠	Pass	Pass	Pass

Opening lead: Jack of hearts.

After North's raise of his demand bid, South leaped directly to slam. He reasoned that the Blackwood convention would
have limited value because of his heart void and that even if
North did have both aces, South couldn't bid a grand slam
with any certainty concerning minor-suit losers.

West opened the heart jack, dummy played the queen, covered by East's king and ruffed by declarer. The spade king
was taken by East and a heart returned.

Declarer made the fine play of ruffing the heart instead of
discarding. He reasoned that a more intelligent discard could
be made after he knew more about the hand. A risky business
against a magician!

Declarer drew the remaining trumps and played his ace and
king of clubs. East followed with the 6 and queen.

Declarer's careful play had apparently materialized. He had
purposely saved his small club instead of discarding it on the
heart ace to cover the possibility that East had originally held
queen and another club.

If so, then four club tricks were available via a finesse
against West's club 10. The diamond finesse would then be

unnecessary, since one diamond could be discarded on the heart ace and the other on the club jack.

Declarer confidently led his club and finessed against West's "marked" club 10. Horrors! Bud Dietrich sprung the trap and cunningly won his club 10 for the setting trick.

Note that if East had not played the club queen, declarer would have had to fall back on the diamond finesse. This would land the slam, since East had the diamond queen.

Anyone care to fill in a foursome with Bud Dietrich?

LEADING AGAINST A SMALL SLAM
"A Thinker's Dream"

Are you happy when the opponents bid a small slam and you are on lead with two aces? Excluding no-trump slams, many an opening leader would have preferred one ace instead of two. Nothing is more painful than leading the wrong ace against a slam!

Today's hand was played several years ago. George Rapee of New York City and the late Bud Smith of Grosse Pointe, Mich., were South and North respectively. The bidding was:

Rapee South	West	Smith North	East
1 ♥	Pass	3 ♥ *	Pass
4 ♥	Pass	5 ♦	Pass
5 ♥	Pass	6 ♣	Pass
6 ♥	Pass	Pass	Pass

*Strong and unlimited.

As West, what would you have led against six hearts?

♠ A 9 7 5 2   ♦ J 9 6
♥ 8 6   ♣ A 7 2

Oswald Jacoby sat West, partnered by Ace Bobby Wolff. Jacoby pondered long and hard over the opening lead. Unusual for such an accurate and lightning-fast thinker.

What were Jacoby's thoughts? Rapee apparently had a minimum hand and no slam interest, since he had signed off in hearts at every opportunity. Bud Smith not only drove the hand to a small slam, his bid of six clubs showed definite interest in a grand slam. In fact, Smith's bidding demanded that

Rapee bid the grand slam if he had first-round spade control.

(When a player cue-bids at the six level, he has in effect, bid a small slam. If his interest were limited to the small slam, he could have bid six in the agreed trump suit. The fact that he cue-bids instead definitely invites a grand slam.)

What could this mean?

The only solution consistent with Jacoby's holding of two black aces was that Smith was void in clubs and had all controls other than the spade ace. (Smith cue-bid clubs but not spades.) Therefore, Jacoby reasoned the only hope for the defense lay in the spade suit.

Since two spade tricks were needed to defeat the contract, Ozzie led the spade deuce!

The entire hand was:

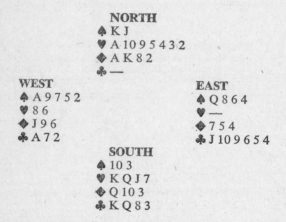

```
                    NORTH
                    ♠ K J
                    ♥ A 10 9 5 4 3 2
                    ♦ A K 8 2
                    ♣ —
    WEST                            EAST
    ♠ A 9 7 5 2                     ♠ Q 8 6 4
    ♥ 8 6                           ♥ —
    ♦ J 9 6                         ♦ 7 5 4
    ♣ A 7 2                         ♣ J 10 9 6 5 4
                    SOUTH
                    ♠ 10 3
                    ♥ K Q J 7
                    ♦ Q 10 3
                    ♣ K Q 8 3
```

Understandably, Rapee played dummy's jack. Who underleads aces against slams? Wolff won the queen and returned a spade to Ozzie's ace. Down one.

Another brilliant maneuver by one of the all-time greats of bridge. Not only did he conclude that no hope existed in the club suit, he correctly analyzed the only play in the spade suit to give Rapee a guess.

Perhaps it is better to choose neither ace when on lead against a small slam? Only if you have as much reason as Jacoby did. However, successful or not, forsaking an ace must be preferable to leading the wrong one!

DIAMONDS FOR DUCHIN
"Musician Makes Sweet Key Play"

Peter Duchin, son of the unforgettable band leader Eddie Duchin, has continued the musical tradition of the family with overwhelming success. His style includes the exciting music of the "Now Generation" and, regardless of individual musical tastes, his sound appeals to all.

Peter began studying music with his father at the age of five. His introduction to bridge came later. He has, however, learned to play an excellent game.

Observe Peter's careful play of today's exciting slam hand. Duchin held the South cards. Cover the East-West cards with your thumbs and plan the play of the slam against the lead of the queen of hearts.

None vulnerable
Dealer North

```
                    NORTH
                    ♠ 10 4
                    ♥ K 7
                    ♦ K Q J 9
                    ♣ Q J 8 4 2
    WEST                              EAST
    ♠ 7                               ♠ Q 8 6 5
    ♥ Q J 10 8 6 2                    ♥ 9 4 3
    ♦ 8 6 2                           ♦ A 7 5
    ♣ K 9 3                           ♣ 10 6 5
                    SOUTH
                    ♠ A K J 9 3 2
                    ♥ A 5
                    ♦ 10 4 3
                    ♣ A 7
```

The bidding:

North	East	South	West
1 ♦	Pass	1 ♠	Pass
2 ♣	Pass	3 ♠	Pass
4 ♣	Pass	6 ♠	Pass
Pass	Pass		

If you were not careful at tricks one and two, you probably lost the slam. Before examining Duchin's play, observe what may happen if South plays carelessly to the first two tricks.

Declarer wins the first heart in dummy to lead the spade 10

for a first-round finesse against East's queen. (This play is better than first playing a high spade to cater to a singleton queen offside.) The spade 10 holds the trick and South continues spades and picks up East's queen.

South next goes after the diamond suit with the intention of establishing the suit and discarding the losing club on the long diamond. However, East foils this plan by refusing to play the ace of diamonds on the first two leads, and declarer is forced into a losing club finesse for down one.

Duchin found the winning line of play. He won the opening heart lead in his hand and immediately played diamonds. East was helpless. If East took the diamond ace, Duchin would have more than enough entries to make the spade finesse and to run the diamonds.

East ducked his diamond ace and Duchin countered by using this entry for the spade finesse. The spade 10 was passed successfully, the finesse was repeated, and trumps were drawn.

Diamonds were established, East ducking until the third round. However, the heart king was still in dummy to provide entry to the fourth diamond.

Note that even after making the correct play of winning the first heart with the ace, any play but the diamond at trick two will lose the slam.

If a high trump is played, East's queen will eventually score a trick. If dummy's heart king is used for the spade finesse, the long diamond will be stranded in dummy.

It was a carefully played hand by Peter Duchin. Obviously he takes the same pains with his slams as he does with his music.

THE MERRIMAC COUP
"Star Billing for La Crawford"

One of the busiest movie stars is actress Joan Crawford. She is the mother of four adopted children, finds time for movie and television appearances, and is a member of the board of directors of the Pepsi-Cola Company and Frito-Lay, Inc. Does she also have time to play cards?

Joan confesses that gin rummy is her best card game. However, we talked her into playing a few hands of bridge on one of her recent visits to Dallas. Observe her defense against today's slam hand. Joan held the East cards.

North-South vulnerable
Dealer South

                        NORTH
                    ♠ Q J 10
                    ♥ 6
                    ♦ Q 8 4 2
                    ♣ A K Q 10 8

    WEST   EAST
    ♠ —   ♠ A 9 4 3
    ♥ K Q J 10 9 7 3   ♥ 8 5 4 2
    ♦ J 9 6   ♦ K 7 5
    ♣ 9 7 5   ♣ J 6

                        SOUTH
                    ♠ K 8 7 6 5 2
                    ♥ A
                    ♦ A 10 3
                    ♣ 4 3 2

The bidding:

South	West	North	East
1 ♠	4 ♥	4 ♠	5 ♥
5 ♠	Pass	6 ♠	Pass
Pass	Pass		

Opening lead: King of hearts.

As is usual with distributional hands, everyone's values tend
to become inflated and the bidding is spirited. However,
South's slam contract is not unreasonable and will actually be
made most of the time.

Typical play might go as follows:

South would win the heart ace and lead to dummy's high
trumps. East would wait until the third round to exhaust dummy's trumps and then hopefully lead a heart. However, declarer would ruff, draw East's last trump and discard two diamonds on dummy's clubs, making six.

There is nothing typical about Joan Crawford. Declarer
won the heart lead and led to dummy's trumps. However,
Joan ducked only once. She now made the only play to defeat
the slam—she returned the diamond king!

Declarer won the ace and faced a Hobson's choice. If he
led a spade to dummy's queen, he would have no entry back
to his hand to draw Joan's last trump. If he played the spade
king, he would establish Joan's 9.

Well planned and well defended.

Joan knew that West must have had seven hearts to justify the four-heart bid. Therefore, there could be no future in that suit. Since dummy's clubs were obviously solid, Joan's only chance lay in the possibility that West held something in diamonds.

Obviously we would be well advised to steer clear of any gin rummy games with Joan Crawford,

SUCCESS OR FAILURE?
"Baer with the Evidence"

Why does one declarer succeed where another fails? Often for the same reason that one lawyer may win a case where another may not. All available evidence must be uncovered and carefully examined.

Observe the brilliant play of today's hand in a recent Swiss team-of-four event (a popular form of international match point team play for large groups).

North-South vulnerable
Dealer East

```
                    NORTH
                  ♠ A 7 2
                  ♥ Q 7 3 2
                  ♦ Q 5 3
                  ♣ 9 3 2
   WEST                              EAST
  ♠ 6 5 4                           ♠ K 9
  ♥ 10 6 5                          ♥ K 8 4
  ♦ K 8 6 2                         ♦ A 10 9 7
  ♣ 8 6 5                           ♣ Q J 10 4
                    SOUTH
                  ♠ Q J 10 8 3
                  ♥ A J 9
                  ♦ J 4
                  ♣ A K 7
```

The bidding:

East	South	West	North
1 ♦	1 ♠	Pass	2 ♠
Pass	4 ♠	Pass	Pass
Pass			

Opening lead: Two of diamonds.

122

The bidding was the same in both rooms and both Souths became declarers in the reasonable contract of four spades.

When the hand was played the first time, East won West's lead of the diamond deuce and shifted to the club queen. South won the king and played the diamond jack. West won and continued clubs. South won his ace and played a spade to dummy's ace. After South's last club was discarded on the diamond queen, he led a low heart from dummy and successfully finessed his jack. When the heart ace failed to drop the king, South went down one, losing one spade, two diamonds and a heart.

When the hand was replayed, Henry Baer, widely known Dallas attorney, was the declarer. The play went exactly the same up to a point. However, after discarding his losing club, instead of taking the heart finesse, Baer ruffed dummy's last club, reducing his hand and dummy to only spades and hearts. A spade was then surrendered to East's blank king and East was forced to concede a ruff and discard or to eliminate Baer's heart loser by leading from the king of hearts.

Why did the declarers part? When East played the spade 9 under the ace, he could have done so under two conditions. One possibility was that he actually held K-9 doubleton. The other possibility was a false card in an attempt to steer declarer from a winning decision in hearts (with a different layout of cards). Baer decided to believe East. He "stuffed" East with the lead and made his contract.

Why did one declarer believe the spade 9 and the other not? The successful declarer, like the successful lawyer, must not only examine the evidence. He must also weigh the credibility of its source.

THE REBID
"The Major or the Minor"

After opening the bidding in a solid five-card major suit, does it pay to rebid the solid suit or is it better to introduce a broken four-card minor suit over an opponent's overcall?

Today's hand, played between France and The Aces in the qualifying rounds of the World Championship, deals with this point. Examine the results achieved through differing choices.

Vulnerable North-South
Dealer East

                        NORTH
                        ♠ 10 3
                        ♥ Q 10 9 7
                        ◆ K J 9 8 2
                        ♣ K 9

    WEST   EAST
    ♠ 9 8 4 2   ♠ 7 5
    ♥ K 8   ♥ A J 6 4 3 2
    ◆ 7 4   ◆ A 3
    ♣ Q J 8 7 6   ♣ 5 3 2

                        SOUTH
                        ♠ A K Q J 6
                        ♥ 5
                        ◆ Q 10 6 5
                        ♣ A 10 4

Open-Room Bidding:

East	South	West	North
Pass	1 ♠	Pass	1 NT
2 ♥	2 ♠	Pass	2 NT
Pass	3 ♥	Dbl.	3 ♠
Pass	4 ◆	Pass	5 ◆
All pass			

Opening lead: Queen of clubs.

Closed-Room Bidding:

East	South	West	North
Pass	1 ♠	Pass	1 NT
2 ♥	3 ◆	Pass	3 NT
All pass			

Open lead: Four of hearts.

In the closed room, South, Jean-Michel Boulenger, decided
to introduce his broken four-card diamond suit at his second
turn to bid. While this action would seem to make it more
probable to play a diamond contract, on this hand, it had
quite the opposite effect. North, Henri Svarc, was faced with a
last-chance choice. He could either bid three no-trump now or
raise diamonds. If he raised diamonds, the opportunity to play
at three no trump would be gone forever.

Unfortunately for France, Svarc chose three no-trump.

East, Ace Jim Jacoby, led his fourth-best heart. It was then a simple matter to clear the suit and wait with the diamond ace to defeat the contract.

In the open room, Ace Bobby Goldman rebid his major suit. Instead of concealing the diamond fit, this choice made possible a scientific investigation of all contracts. Over the two-spade rebid, Ace Mike Lawrence was able to suggest a no-trump contract without a firm commitment. Over two no-trump, Goldman (South) made a waiting cue bid of three hearts which West doubled to show something in the suit. Lawrence (North) showed a tepid preference for spades and when Goldman finally bid the diamonds at the four level Lawrence's choice of contracts was clear.

At five diamonds the play was routine. South lost a diamond and a heart and made his contract easily.

Is it better to rebid the solid major? On this hand it certainly was. Even though game was on in the broken minor!

One of bridge's many paradoxes: one player bids diamonds at his first opportunity only to miss game in the suit. The other player ignores diamonds but ends in the contract anyway. Finally, regardless of what rebid was chosen, the four-spade game was not reached at either table.

PLANNING THE PLAY
"The Jack That Shouldn't Have Stayed in the Box"

This deal was one of the most interesting hands of the 1970 world championship. Ace Bob Hamman, playing with Mike Lawrence, had a chance to demonstrate two of his qualities: He likes to bid to the limit. Then he likes to play hard to justify his optimism. The Aces' opponent was Taiwan.

All vulnerable
Dealer South

```
                    NORTH
                    ♠ 5 4 2
                    ♥ A 4 3
                    ◆ Q 8 6
                    ♣ K 8 5 3
        WEST                        EAST
        ♠ K Q 10 8 6                ♠ J 9 7
        ♥ J 2                       ♥ 9 6
        ◆ J 7 4                     ◆ K 10 5 3 2
        ♣ A J 4                     ♣ Q 10 6
                    SOUTH
                    ♠ A 3
                    ♥ K Q 10 8 7 5
                    ◆ A 9
                    ♣ 9 7 2
```

The bidding:

Hamman	Lin	Lawrence	Hsiao
South	**West**	**North**	**East**
1 ♥	1 ♠	2 ♥	2 ♠
4 ♥	Pass	Pass	Pass

West opened the spade king, which was ducked and the
spade continuation taken by the ace. Bob studied hard. What
was he thinking?

He had two chances. The first required both diamond king
and club ace with West. If so, Bob could play the ace and another diamond, establishing the queen. Later he could discard
a club loser on the diamond queen. A club lead to the king
would limit his losers to one trick in each side suit.

Not a bad plan. However, if this were to have any chance,
what did East have to justify his spade raise? Exit old plan,
enter new.

East was presumed to have at least one of the missing key
cards. If it was the club ace, there was no play. East's key
card had to be the diamond king.

Bob concluded that the only legitimate way to make the
hand was to establish dummy's fourth club for a discard of
his own diamond loser. To succeed, clubs must divide evenly and the club ace be with West. What else?

He must keep West from attacking diamonds! Since East
could not safely attack the diamond suit, Bob had to sneak a
club trick into East. This would provide the timing to estab-

lish the fourth club.

Bob played the club 7 at trick three (drawing trumps was delayed to withold information from West and to provide an entry to the established club). West ducked and the hand was over!

East saw what was coming and attacked diamonds. However, Bob had his mind made up and allowed the diamond to run to dummy's queen.

The contract would have been defeated if West had covered the club 7 with his jack. West could then gain the lead in clubs and attack diamonds while East still had a club entry and before the fourth club was established. (The play of the club ace on the 7 and an attack on diamonds will fail. Declarer can establish a diamond in dummy for a club discard.)

Now it is easy to see that West should have covered with the jack. However, this was far from clear at the table. South could easily have had the Q-10-7 of clubs.

After the match Bob was heard to say:

"If he had covered, my plan would have been for naught. Not only that. I would have had to stop stretching my bids. The captain and coach were both watching!"

CHOICE OF CONTRACTS
"Nine Tricks Came Home—Ten Was Too Many!"

One of the most difficult of all areas of bidding is knowing whether the combined potential of your hand and your partner's is nine or ten tricks.

When the fit is in a major, the tendency is to gamble for game in the major. Every so often a contract of three no-trump will be best even with the major suit fit. How does one decide whether to play a close game in a major or in no-trump? Experience, intuition, distribution and a little luck are involved.

Here we have a little of each as Ace Bobby Goldman comes up with just the right bid at just the right time in an important match against a strong New York team.

East-West vulnerable
Dealer North

EISENBERG
NORTH
♠ K 5 3
♥ K 10 9 6 5 4
♦ 10 7
♣ Q 8

WEST
♠ J 9 6
♥ 8 3 2
♦ K J 9 8
♣ A K 6

EAST
♠ Q 10 8 7
♥ J
♦ Q 6 2
♣ J 10 7 5 2

GOLDMAN
SOUTH
♠ A 4 2
♥ A Q 7
♦ A 5 4 3
♣ 9 4 3

The bidding:

North	East	South	West
2 ♥	Pass	2 NT	Pass
3 ♥	Pass	3 NT	Pass
Pass	Pass		

Opening lead: Eight of diamonds.

First a review of the bidding. Billy Eisenberg, sitting North, opened the bidding with a weak two bid. The two-heart bid showed a good six-card suit and not quite enough to open the bidding with one heart.

Bobby Goldman, looking at the South hand, could count six quick heart tricks and two aces for eight, and that was counting on only three high-card points from his partner. Goldman tried two no-trump, a bid that asked Eisenberg for more information.

Eisenberg rebid three hearts to show no additional values. Now Goldman was certain that the combined hands would not produce ten tricks in hearts. However, rather than give up on game altogether, he decided that three no-trump would be a good gamble, particularly if a club would not be led!

Having concealed his strength and stoppers, Goldman opted for the nine-trick game contract. Billy Grieve, sitting West, was on opening lead and decided to lead fourth best from his longest and strongest, just as you and I would usually do. Only it didn't work this time.

Given the diamond lead, Goldman raced off the first nine tricks without ever looking back. Had Grieve led the king of clubs instead, the hand would have been defeated one trick with the existing 5-3 club division.

Notice that if clubs were 4-4, no lead could have defeated three no-trump, and four hearts has no play at all. Playing in hearts, declarer would take the same nine tricks Goldman took at no-trump but would not get the game bonus.

Lucky? Perhaps. But luck comes only to those who seek it.

DECEPTIVE PLAY
"That Wily Jack of Diamonds"

The world of tournament bridge provides many stimulants to the emotions. At different times, sometimes in rapid succession, the intense competitor experiences joy and sorrow, pride and humility, love and hate, joy and laughter, and, too rarely, compassion.

To the competitor, as important as the event itself, is the exchange of humorous or "look at what happened to me" tales. Mutual exchange of these tales probably make many a visit to the psychiatrist's couch unnecessary.

Today's hand concerns one of the sad stories.

North-South vulnerable
Dealer South

```
                    NORTH
                    ♠ A 3
                    ♥ 9 3 2
                    ♦ Q 10 9 8
                    ♣ A K 10 8
    WEST                            EAST
    ♠ 8 2                           ♠ 10 9 7 5 4
    ♥ A Q J 7 5 4                   ♥ 10 8
    ♦ 7 6 2                         ♦ K J
    ♣ 3 2                           ♣ 7 6 5 4
                    SOUTH
                    ♠ K Q J 6
                    ♥ K 6
                    ♦ A 5 4 3
                    ♣ Q J 9
```

The bidding:

South	West	North	East
1 NT	2 ♥	3 NT	Pass
Pass	Pass		

Opening lead: Two of diamonds.

Sitting North-South were two winning players who, until this hand, were enjoying a fine session. Sitting East and West were a bridge teacher (Bobby Wolff) and one of his pupils taking a playing lesson. This was her first tournament.

The bidding was uneventful, and the experts quickly reached three no-trump. Wolff made the best lead. He selected a diamond instead of a lead from his long suit. This was ideal for the defense since it found East's entry and prevented South from scoring his heart king.

Declarer didn't like this lead. It looked like he was headed for a poor score. (He didn't know how poor!) Without the heart lead he might be held to only nine tricks. At other tables, a heart lead would allow other declarers to take ten tricks instead of nine.

Sorrowfully, South played low from dummy. East followed with the *king* (!!). South's eyes flashed like floodlights! Do you see what he saw?

Declarer now saw twelve tricks instead of ten. Four spades, four clubs, and four diamonds (the "marked" finesse against West's diamond jack).

South greedily captured East's king and quickly rattled off four top spades. Joyfully, he led the diamond 5, saving the clubs for entries to repeat the diamond finesse.

West followed with the 6 and South finessed dummy's 9 with confidence. East played the jack and was greatly surprised to find she had won the trick! She recovered in time to remember West's heart bid. She led the heart 10 and South turned green as he gasped for air. The defense quickly gathered six heart tricks and South was down three.

"That was quite a diamond play," said Bobby Wolff. "Thank you," said the bewildered but obviously pleased pupil. "You told me to always play third hand high."

Down three made the expert hate himself for his greed. The conversation made him hate the entire world.

"Shearing Billy the Kid"

Two of the world's most highly respected bridge players are Giorgio Belladonna and Benito Garozzo. In a seven-week, seven-city exhibition tour of the United States and Canada, The Aces got to know this pair both at and away from the bridge table. To say that we were impressed would be an understatement. As individuals in separate partnerships, they were great. As a partnership, they were superb.

Witness Giorgio's play of the following hand played in Winnipeg, Canada.

North-South vulnerable
Dealer West

```
                    NORTH
                    ♠ 7 6 5 2
                    ♥ K 6 2
                    ♦ J 6 3
                    ♣ K Q 3
     WEST                              EAST
     ♠ K J 9 4                        ♠ 8 3
     ♥ Q J 5 4                        ♥ 10 8
     ♦ 10 4                           ♦ 5 2
     ♣ 10 5 2                         ♣ A J 9 8 7 6 4
                    SOUTH
                    ♠ A Q 10
                    ♥ A 9 7 3
                    ♦ A K Q 9 8 7
                    ♣ —
```

The bidding:

Eisenberg	Delmouly	Goldman	Belladonna
West	**North**	**East**	**South**
Pass	Pass	4 ♣	5 ♣
Pass	5 NT	Pass	6 ♦
Pass	Pass	Pass	

Opening lead: Two of clubs.

Goldman's preemptive opening of four clubs duplicated Garozzo's bid in the other room. Belladonna's five-club cue bid showed a massive hand, asking his partner to pick a trump suit. Delmouly bid five no-trump to show strength in the club suit and no strong preference for any suit. Giorgio bid the

131

slam in diamonds, hoping that dummy would have a few cards of value.

Eisenberg led the club deuce, covered by the queen, ace and ruffed.

The apparent line of play for six diamonds is to play one high trump, play ace and king of hearts, discard the spade 10 on the club king and then play a third round of hearts.

If hearts break three-three, a diamond to the jack and a successful spade finesse will bring in the contract. If hearts do not break, the fourth heart can be ruffed with the diamond jack and the same spade finesse taken. Really not an unreasonable line of play and the one adopted in the other room. (Circus preempts are usually stronger, making the spade finesse a very reasonable possibility.)

Here's how Belladonna played the hand. After the club ruff, he played three rounds of trumps ending in dummy. His spade 10 was discarded on the king of clubs and a club ruffed. When Giorgio's last trump was played, this was the position:

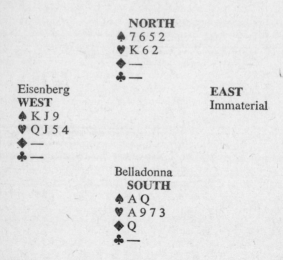

NORTH
♠ 7 6 5 2
♥ K 6 2
♦ —
♣ —

Eisenberg
WEST
♠ K J 9
♥ Q J 5 4
♦ —
♣ —

EAST
Immaterial

Belladonna
SOUTH
♠ A Q
♥ A 9 7 3
♦ Q
♣ —

If Eisenberg discarded a spade, Giorgio would play the A-Q of spades, establishing dummy's third and fourth spades, using the heart king as an entry. If Eisenberg discarded a heart, Giorgio would play ace, king, and another heart. West would be forced to lead a spade into the A-Q and Giorgio's fourth heart would be established.

All this took place in full view of eight hundred bridge fans

132

through closed-circuit television. Like the Canadian Mounties, Giorgio knew he had his man and could not hide his elation. Eisenberg looked as though he was surrounded by the Mounted Police.

A superbly played hand by a truly great player.

INTERFERENCE BIDDING
"A High-Hearted Hand"

A key hand of the final rounds of the 1970 world championship resulted in a grand slam bid being made in one room while a small slam was defeated in the other. The result was a mammoth gain of 2,240 points or 19 IMPs.

All vulnerable
Dealer South

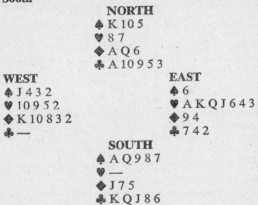

```
                    NORTH
                  ♠ K 10 5
                  ♥ 8 7
                  ◆ A Q 6
                  ♣ A 10 9 5 3
WEST                              EAST
♠ J 4 3 2                         ♠ 6
♥ 10 9 5 2                        ♥ A K Q J 6 4 3
◆ K 10 8 3 2                      ◆ 9 4
♣ —                              ♣ 7 4 2
                    SOUTH
                  ♠ A Q 9 8 7
                  ♥ —
                  ◆ J 7 5
                  ♣ K Q J 8 6
```

Closed-room bidding:

Hsiao	Hamman	Lin	Lawrence
South	**West**	**North**	**East**
1 ♠	Pass	2 ♣	2 ♥
3 ♥	4 ♥	5 ♥	Pass
6 ♣	6 ♥	6 ♠	Pass
Pass	Pass		

In the closed room, the bidding was spirited, with every player bidding the heart suit at least once. It was difficult for North to make a good bid over West's six hearts. A pass was out because this would promise first-round heart control and imply a willingness to play seven clubs. A double had to be wrong.

Six spades was the most reasonable compromise.

Hamman saw no future in leading hearts and selected a diamond instead. On the bidding, this was a very reasonable lead. It turned out to be the only lead to give declarer a chance.

However, declarer feared a diamond or club ruff and played the ace. If trumps divided, or if East had the four trumps, South would have scored the slam without risking a ruff. He was unlucky; down one.

In the open room, the bidding was:

Jacoby **South**	Tai **West**	Wolff **North**	Huang **East**
2 ♣	Pass	2 ♦	3 ♥
3 ♠	4 ♥	6 ♣	6 ♥
Pass	Pass	7 ♣	Pass
Pass	Pass		

Jacoby's two-club opening showed clubs, possibly another suit, 12-16 points. Wolff's two-diamond bid asked clarification. After East's preemptive attempt, Jacoby's three-spade bid identified a club-spade two-suiter.

Wolff's six clubs was based on general strength and hopes that Jacoby had a heart singleton. East's bid of six hearts changed things completely.

In the other room, it was West who had bid six hearts! With first-round heart control, Jacoby was able to pass the six-heart bid and allow Wolff to make the final decision. Wolff confidently bid the grand slam.

Jacoby ran into the same bad luck in the spade suit; otherwise, the grand slam could be claimed (five spades, five clubs, diamond ace and two diamond ruffs). As it turned out, Jacoby threw one diamond from dummy on his fifth spade and took the successful diamond finesse for the grand slam.

The Aces were in top form throughout the championship. As in this hand, maximum pressure was applied continuously. When a team loses 19 IMPs on one hand, usually some crime is committed. However, you be the judge.

Did the Chinese lose 19 IMPs because of bad play? Consider also that even if six spades had succeeded, The Aces still would have picked up 710 points or 12 IMPs!

A CHOICE BETWEEN LOSING TRICKS
"Safe Tortoise Beats Flashy Hare"

At all levels of play, the secret of success lies not so much in playing well as in not playing badly—quite a different thing. The opportunity for brilliance presents itself rarely; the opportunity for error lies around every corner.

Today's hand was played in an important match for the European Championships. It serves to demonstrate the type of careless mistake that loses not only important matches but the at-home foursome as well.

North-South vulnerable
Dealer South

```
                        NORTH
                        ♠ Q 8 6 4 3
                        ♥ K 5 3
                        ♦ K Q 7 2
                        ♣ 5
       WEST                             EAST
       ♠ A K 10 2                       ♠ J 9 5
       ♥ 9                              ♥ Q J 6
       ♦ J 10 9 8                       ♦ 6 5 4 3
       ♣ Q 10 7 3                       ♣ A K 2
                        SOUTH
                        ♠ 7
                        ♥ A 10 8 7 4 2
                        ♦ A
                        ♣ J 9 8 6 4
```

The bidding:

South	West	North	East
Pass	Pass	1 ♠	Pass
3 ♥	Pass	4 ♥	Pass
Pass	Pass		

Opening lead: Jack of diamonds

The aggressive heart game was reached in both rooms after South's jump shift, which, after an original pass, was forcing for one round.

The first declarer won the opening lead with his diamond ace, quickly led to dummy's heart king, and discarded his losing spade on the diamond king. He succeeded in avoiding a spade loser, but he could no longer avoid the loss of three club tricks and a trump trick (East leading trumps at each opportunity). Down one.

When the hand was replayed, Joel Tarlo of Great Britain did not play brilliantly. He merely avoided playing badly. After the same lead of the diamond jack, he took the time to count his losers. He resisted the temptation to quickly discard his losing spade and played as follows.

After winning the diamond ace, he led a club from his hand. West won the trick, cashed the spade king and led a trump. Declarer ducked in dummy and captured East's jack with the ace. A club was ruffed in dummy with a low trump and two clubs were discarded on the high diamonds.

A spade was ruffed back to the South hand, and another club was ruffed with dummy's heart king. South then conceded a trick to the high trump and made his contract, losing one spade, one club and one trump.

As this hand demonstrates, careless play occurs at all levels. While Tarlo's line of play was not brilliant, nor was it impregnable against all distributions, it was certainly better than the impulsive play made at the other table. A good lesson for all declarers.

HOLD-UP PLAY
"The Calm before the Storm"

Gale Storm, as a star of television, motion pictures, records, stage and night clubs, enjoys a most interesting and diversified career. Her first television show "My Little Margie," made her one of the nation's top television stars. As a change of pace, she scored a gold record with her first record, "I Hear You Knocking."

On a recent visit to Dallas, where she starred on stage in "Cactus Flower," Miss Storm graciously accepted an invitation from The Aces for a few hands of bridge and quickly demonstrated that her potential was not limited to the entertainment field.

Witness her defense of today's hand from the West position.

Both vulnerable
Dealer North

                        NORTH
                        ♠ K
                        ♥ 8 2
                        ♦ K Q J 3
                        ♣ K Q J 8 7 6

        WEST   EAST
        ♠ J 9 8 6 3   ♠ Q 10 7 5 4 2
        ♥ A 6 3   ♥ 5
        ♦ 10 7 6 2   ♦ A 9 8 4
        ♣ 5   ♣ 4 3

                        SOUTH
                        ♠ A
                        ♥ K Q J 10 9 7 4
                        ♦ 5
                        ♣ A 10 9 2

The bidding:

North	East	South	West
1 ♣	Pass	2 ♥	Pass
3 ♣	Pass	4 NT	Pass
5 ♣	Pass	5 ♥	All pass

Opening lead: Five of clubs.

Over North's opening bid of one club, South justifiably
made a jump shift and then launched into Blackwood to
check on aces. Unfortunately, North showed none and South
had to settle in five hearts.

Miss Storm selected the lead of her singleton club. It was a
fine choice, since her heart ace gave her control of the trump
suit.

Declarer won the club in dummy and led a heart to the
king, enticing Miss Storm to win her ace. She made the excellent play of refusing the trick!

She reasoned that if she took the trick, she had only a 50-
50 chance of guessing which side ace her partner held (the
bidding had made it obvious that South was missing two
aces).

Declarer continued trumps and Miss Storm took her ace.
Her patience was rewarded when East showed out and sig-
naled vigorously with the diamond 9. It was now easy to lead
a diamond to East for the club ruff. Down one.

Patience and clear thinking won for Gale Storm.

THE GAMBLE FOR THE ODDS
"Here's to the Men Who Lose!"

The winning player tries to play with the odds. While the laws of probability do not guarantee the results of any given hand, it pays to play with the probabilities in the long run. However, even to players who fully understand this, improbable events can sometimes be very frustrating.

Witness the frustrations of today's hand played in the 1971 World Championship between North America II and Taiwan. Richard Walsh of Los Angeles was the unlucky declarer (South).

North-South vulnerable
Dealer North

```
                    NORTH
                    ♠ 10 8
                    ♥ 9 6
                    ♦ Q 10 4 3
                    ♣ K Q 5 3 2
     WEST                          EAST
     ♠ J                           ♠ 9 7 6 3
     ♥ J 7 4 2                     ♥ A 10 5 3
     ♦ K 9 6 2                     ♦ 8 5
     ♣ A 10 7 6                    ♣ 9 8 4
                    SOUTH
                    ♠ A K Q 5 4 2
                    ♥ K Q 8
                    ♦ A J 7
                    ♣ J
```

The bidding:

North	East	South	West
Pass	Pass	2 ♣	Pass
2 ♦	Pass	2 ♠	Pass
3 ♣	Pass	3 ♠	Pass
4 ♦	Pass	4 ♠	All pass

Opening lead: Two of diamonds.

South opened with an all-purpose forcing bid of two clubs, and, over the negative (or waiting) two-diamond response, made the game forcing bid of two spades. South became declarer in the spade game after North bid both his minor suits.

West led the diamond deuce, dummy holding the trick with

the queen. Declarer reasoned that the most likely course to success was to play for the loss of only one heart trick. If so, all that would be needed was the almost 70 percent chance of an even spade division to limit his losses to one in each side suit.

Accordingly, declarer led a low heart from dummy. He deferred playing trumps so that he would be able to ruff a heart in dummy if necessary. East ducked the heart ace and declarer won the queen. Staying with his plan, declarer continued with hearts, playing the 8 from his hand.

East won the 10 and led a diamond. Declarer won the ace and ruffed his heart king in dummy. He was now ready to draw trumps and claim, conceding a club and a diamond. He received a rude shock when spades broke badly and East turned up with a trump trick.

If declarer had played for the highly improbable layout which actually existed, he would have made an overtrick. After winning the diamond queen, a club to his jack would drive out West's ace. Dummy's king and queen would take care of declarer's small diamond and small heart. Since West held a singleton jack of trumps, the trump suit could be handled with no losers and the trump 10 would provide an entry to the good clubs.

North America II lost 760 points on this deal, the opponents playing three no-trump and making five in the other room. Did Walsh play in accordance with the odds? A very complex question. However, he did adopt a very reasonable line of play and certainly not one that should cost so much.

DENYING THE OBVIOUS
"The Lady Takes a Second Look"

Joan Blumofe, daughter of the ageless Jack Benny, learned her bridge during the period her father was 39 years old. Consequently, she found enough time to learn her way around the bridge table.

Witness Joan's play of today's interesting game hand.

Both vulnerable
Dealer South

NORTH
♠ A 9 8 3
♥ 9 3
♦ A K 6 4 2
♣ 10 6

WEST
♠ Q J 10 6
♥ Q 8 4 2
♦ J 9
♣ A 7 2

EAST
♠ K 7 4 2
♥ 7 6
♦ Q 10 7 3
♣ 8 5 3

SOUTH
♠ 5
♥ A K J 10 5
♦ 8 5
♣ K Q J 9 4

The bidding:

South	West	North	East
1 ♥	Pass	2 ♦	Pass
2 ♥	Pass	2 ♠	Pass
3 ♣	Pass	3 ♥	Pass
4 ♥	Pass	Pass	Pass

Opening lead: Queen of spades

South decided to open with one heart rather than one club because of the excellent texture of the heart suit—and the 100 honors! After North showed a preference for hearts over clubs, South bid the heart game.

Play to the first trick was easy. West's lead of the spade queen was won by dummy's ace. Before playing the second trick, however, declarer took time out for a second look.

Observe what would have happened had declarer taken the obvious heart finesse. West would win the queen and lead another spade. Declarer would be forced to ruff, reducing herself to the same number of trumps held by West. Whether or not declarer pulled trumps, she would not have been able to make the hand. West would gain the lead with the club ace and either force another ruff or, if declarer had chosen to draw trumps, West could cash two spade tricks.

Joan's second look catered to the existing situation. Instead of taking the obvious trump finesse, she played both her high trumps. When the queen failed to drop, she abandoned the trump suit to drive out the club ace.

A low club was won by dummy's 10 and a low club to South's jack was taken by the ace. A spade lead forced South to ruff; however, the club suit was now established. South continued to play her good clubs and West scored both the queen and 8 of trumps. However, South retained control of the hand and lost only three tricks—one club and two trumps.

Joan Blumofe's play deliberately gave up any chance of losing only one trump trick. Even if trumps had divided evenly, she would have lost two trump tricks. However, she correctly decided that making the contract was more important than a possible overtrick.

THE WRONG GUESS
"Mathe Makes a Tough Decision— Then Takes It on the Chin"

The 1971 World Championship started with both North American teams playing each other in the first round. The Aces, defending champions, played against North America II, a team including Lew Mathe, Don Krauss, Dick Walsh, and John Swanson, all of Los Angeles, and two leading East Coast players, Edgar Kaplan of New York City and Norman Kay of Philadelphia.

After the first few boards, North America II jumped off to a substantial 32-0 lead against The Aces. However, The Aces surged back to lead by a half-time score of 59-41 IMPs, and in the second half, The Aces scored heavily and won the match 98-50 IMPs.

Today's hand helped turn the tide in favor of The Aces.

Both vulnerable
Dealer East

NORTH
♠ A 7 5 4
♥ 10 9 6 4 3
♦ —
♣ K 9 6 2

WEST
♠ K Q 9
♥ K Q 8 2
♦ J 2
♣ A 8 7 3

EAST
♠ J 10 8 6 3 2
♥ J 7
♦ A 8 7
♣ Q 5

SOUTH
♠ —
♥ A 5
♦ K Q 10 9 6 5 4 3
♣ J 10 4

The bidding:

East	South	West	North
Pass	1 ♦		
2 ♠	5 ♦	Dbl.	1 ♥
		All pass	

Opening lead: King of spades.

When Aces Jim Jacoby and Bobby Wolff held the North-South cards, the bidding went as shown. At Wolff's (South) second turn, he decided to leap directly to five diamonds. This bid silenced the opponents as neither one had a clear-cut course.

The play was quick. Wolff won the opening lead with the spade ace and discarded his losing heart. He crossed to his ace of hearts to play the diamond king, taken by East. Wolff ruffed the spade return and the diamond queen felled the jack. Wolff drew the other trump and success rested on the location of the club queen. This was offside and the contract was down one.

When the hand was replayed, Ace Bob Hamman (East) became the declarer at a doubled four-spade contract after this bidding:

East	South	West	North
Pass	1 ♦	Dbl.	1 ♥
2 ♠	3 ♦	3 ♠	Pass
4 ♠	Pass	Pass	Dbl.
All pass			

South opened the diamond king and after dummy followed low, North (Lew Mathe) had a difficult decision. If South had led from the A-K of diamonds, it appeared that the best chance to defeat the contract lay in the defense taking two diamond tricks in addition to the spade ace and the club king. Therefore, Mathe discarded a club on the diamond king.

East won the diamond ace and led hearts driving out the ace. South cashed the diamond queen and led another. However, dummy ruffed with a spade honor, and declarer led trumps and later discarded his club loser on the good heart. Making four, doubled and 790 points to The Aces.

Had Mathe guessed to ruff the diamond king, he could have defeated the hand by putting South on lead with the heart ace for another diamond ruff. A very tough decision and a severe penalty to pay for guessing wrong.

USING A SMALL SINGLETON TRUMP
"Resist the Ruff—Make It Tough"

A defender can find few useful purposes for a singleton small trump. It's usually one of the first cards he must play and about the best he can hope for is the rare opportunity to hurt declarer's chances by ruffing one of declarer's winners. Even more rare, however, is the opportunity to hurt declarer by refusing to ruff.

Follow the defense of today's hand by Ace Mike Lawrence (East). The hand was played against France in the qualifying rounds of the 1971 World Championship.

Both vulnerable
Dealer South

```
                    NORTH
                    ♠ A J
                    ♥ A 9 7 3
                    ◆ 8 2
                    ♣ J 9 6 5 3
        WEST                        EAST
        ♠ K 10 6                    ♠ 9 8 4 3 2
        ♥ Q 5 4                     ♥ 6
        ◆ J 10 5                    ◆ A Q 7 4 3
        ♣ A Q 4 2                   ♣ 10 8
                    SOUTH
                    ♠ Q 7 5
                    ♥ K J 10 8 2
                    ◆ K 9 6
                    ♣ K 7
```

The bidding:

Roudinesco	Goldman	Stoppa	Lawrence
South	**West**	**North**	**East**
1 ♥	Pass	4 ♥	All pass

Opening lead: Jack of diamonds.

North rejected the slow and easy approach and, instead, jumped directly to the heart game. At IMP scoring, failure to seize the slightest excuse to bid any vulnerable game is considered by many to be a felony.

West led the diamond jack and East won the ace. East shifted to the club 10, declarer ducked, and West won the queen. West then cashed the club ace for the third defensive trick and at the same time, established all of dummy's remaining clubs.

Declarer's problem now centered on the trump suit. Since he could discard two spades on two of the established clubs, the spade finesse was no longer necessary.

After winning the club ace, West shifted to a spade and declarer won dummy's ace. Needing only two of dummy's clubs for discards, declarer decided to tempt East into ruffing one of dummy's clubs. In that manner, declarer might improve his chances at locating the trump queen.

The club jack was played enticingly from dummy and Lawrence nonchalantly discarded a spade. Declarer also discarded a spade. Declarer played another club from dummy to test Lawrence once again. Again an unconcerned discard. Declarer discarded his last spade loser and was left with only the problem in trumps.

Declarer reasoned, "How could anyone resist ruffing a winner if he held only small trumps? Ergo, East must be protecting the trump queen."

Declarer played dummy's trump ace intending to finesse against East's queen if necessary. When East discarded on the second trump lead, the ruse was exposed but not in time to save the contract.

A most rare and exciting defensive coup.

SUPERIOR DEFENSE
"Forget the Tea Leaves and the Crystal Ball—
It's in the Cards"

I asked Ace Bobby Wolff about his favorite hand of the
World Championship. He did not equivocate. One hand stood
head and shoulders above the rest. Believe it or not, it was a
part-score contract played in the qualifying rounds against
Australia. No one vulnerable to boot!

Vulnerable 0
Dealer North

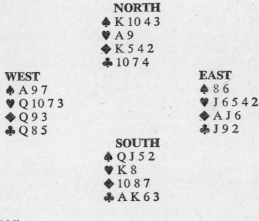

NORTH
♠ K 10 4 3
♥ A 9
♦ K 5 4 2
♣ 10 7 4

WEST
♠ A 9 7
♥ Q 10 7 3
♦ Q 9 3
♣ Q 8 5

EAST
♠ 8 6
♥ J 6 5 4 2
♦ A J 6
♣ J 9 2

SOUTH
♠ Q J 5 2
♥ K 8
♦ 10 8 7
♣ A K 6 3

The bidding:

North	East	South	West
Pass	Pass	1 ♠	Pass
3 ♠	Pass	Pass	Pass

Opening lead: Seven of spades.

After North had passed, Wolff opened the South hand with
one spade and Jim Jacoby (North) raised to three spades.
Since Wolff's hand was minimum, he declined the invitation
and passed. A wise choice.

West opened the trump 7 which was won by South's jack.
South continued with another trump which was won by
West's ace. West then exited with the heart 3, won in dummy
by the ace. Declarer played the spade king to draw the remaining trumps and was now at the crossroads.

"What were your thoughts?" I asked.

"I was wishing I were playing two spades instead of three! When West showed up with the spade ace, I felt sure that the diamond ace was with East. If so, it was going to be difficult to avoid losing a spade, three diamonds, and a club, and the contract."

"How did you decide?" I continued.

"I had some chance if clubs were divided evenly. If so, I could play my heart king, eliminating hearts from my hand and dummy, and then play three rounds of clubs, forcing the defenders to lead diamonds for me. The problem was that if clubs did not divide, a fourth round of clubs would put me in dummy and I would be forced to lead away from the king of diamonds."

Wolff played for the even club division and when West won the club queen, this was the position:

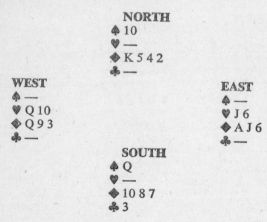

```
                    NORTH
                    ♠ 10
                    ♥ —
                    ♦ K 5 4 2
                    ♣ —
    WEST                            EAST
    ♠ —                             ♠ —
    ♥ Q 10                          ♥ J 6
    ♦ Q 9 3                         ♦ A J 6
    ♣ —                             ♣ —
                    SOUTH
                    ♠ Q
                    ♥ —
                    ♦ 10 8 7
                    ♣ 3
```

West, sensing the problem involved play of the diamond suit, led the diamond queen hoping to convince Wolff that he also held the jack. Wolff covered with the king and East won with the ace. To continue the excellent defense, East led the diamond 6. The play of the jack would have established the 10 and eliminated all problems.

Wolff had to choose between a finesse against the diamond 9 or the existing card combination. He diagnosed the hand perfectly and rose with the 10 to make the contract.

Superior defense countered at every turn by accurate card reading. No wonder this hand sticks in Bobby Wolff's mind!

PROTHRO WAS PREPARED
"From Bear to Ram—Lion Becomes a Lamb"

Tommy Prothro, one of America's most successful college coaches for many years (UCLA Bruins), coaches professional football now. He is now the head coach of the Los Angeles Rams. Prothro has always been a popular sports figure, a shrewd tactician and one who believes in being prepared.

Preparedness in bridge is as important as in football. Witness how Prothro applied this principle in the play of today's interesting game hand.

East-West vulnerable
Dealer North

```
                    NORTH
                    ♠ A 5
                    ♥ 10 6
                    ◆ 10 9 6 3
                    ♣ A K 7 5 3
   WEST                              EAST
   ♠ 10 9 6 4                        ♠ 8 3
   ♥ J 7 2                           ♥ A K Q 8 4
   ◆ Q 8 5 2                         ◆ J 7 4
   ♣ J 4                             ♣ Q 10 9
                    SOUTH
                    ♠ K Q J 7 2
                    ♥ 9 5 3
                    ◆ A K
                    ♣ 8 6 2
```

The bidding:

North	East	South	West
1 ♣	1 ♥	1 ♠	Pass
2 ♣	Pass	3 ♠	Pass
4 ♠	All pass		

Opening lead. Two of hearts.

The bidding was standard, with North responding to South's forcing bids by first rebidding his club suit and then raising to the spade game.

West led the heart deuce and East's queen won the trick. East made the excellent shift to a trump which Prothro won in dummy with the ace. Prothro now made the unusual play

147

of a low club from dummy! What was he up to?

Examine the course of the play had Prothro not made this play.

If Prothro had drawn trumps and then played to establish clubs, the defense could take three hearts and one club. If Prothro had led another heart, East would win and lead another trump. This would exhaust dummy's trumps, and when declarer tried to establish clubs he would lose the same three hearts and one club. And finally, if he had played A-K and another club, he would have established the clubs, but he would have never been able to use them.

Prothro's play established dummy's clubs while he still retained control of the hand. Regardless of which defender won the trick, Prothro's losses were limited to two hearts and one club. In actual play, East won the club queen and cashed a high heart. Prothro won the diamond shift, drew trumps and claimed the balance. In all, he lost two hearts and one club.

A fine example of preparedness. Any guesses on whether Prothro's Rams will be prepared for the coming season?

PRECISION PLAY
"Showmanship a Natural to Big Top Promoter"

"The Greatest Show on Earth" was in Dallas recently and the Ringling Bros., Barnum & Bailey Circus boasted all the attractions of days gone by. Only the Big Top, the other tents, the vans and the smell of crushed grass were missing as Dallas' modern air-conditioned auditorium housed the show.

Don Hintz, today's version of the busy promoter with the long black cigar and long handlebar mustache, and the man responsible for all phases of staging the show, somehow finds time to play an excellent game of bridge. Witness his trapeze act in the play of today's interesting game contract.

Both vulnerable
Dealer West

NORTH
- ♠ A 9 3
- ♥ 8 5 3
- ♦ 8 6 2
- ♣ J 10 9 5

WEST
- ♠ 5
- ♥ K J 9 4
- ♦ J 10 3
- ♣ A K Q 7 2

EAST
- ♠ 7 4
- ♥ 10 7 2
- ♦ K Q 9 5
- ♣ 8 6 4 3

SOUTH
- ♠ K Q J 10 8 6 2
- ♥ A Q 6
- ♦ A 7 4
- ♣ —

The bidding:

West	North	East	South
1 ♣	Pass	2 ♣	4 ♠
Pass	Pass	Pass	

Opening lead: King of clubs.

Hintz saw no point in any fancy bidding after East's raise to two clubs and ended the auction with his leap to the spade game. Certainly a reasonable gamble.

Routine play would have lost the hand. The heart finesse would not succeed and declarer would have lost two hearts and two diamonds for down one.

There is nothing routine about the circus nor about Hintz. In the center ring he started the act by ruffing West's lead of the club king with his 6 of spades, carefully saving his deuce.

He led his spade king and overtook with dummy's ace. Dummy's club jack came next and instead of ruffing, declarer discarded a diamond. West won and shifted the attack to diamonds. Declarer won the diamond ace and entered dummy by leading his spade 8 to dummy's 9.

The club 10 was played and declarer threw his last diamond. West won the trick and dummy's club 9 was established. West continued with a diamond which Hintz ruffed high, once again holding on to his deuce.

Hintz then completed the performance with a display of showmanship. His spade deuce to dummy's spade three gave him a vital entry. Dummy's 9 of clubs took care of declarer's small heart and the contract was secure. The losing heart finesse was for a possible overtrick.

Hintz's play involved two major acts. A repeated loser on loser play in clubs plus careful manipulation of entries in the trump suit. Almost as much fun as watching the trapeze act and the tight rope simultaneously.

HIGH BIDS BY VULNERABLE OPPONENTS
"What Are They Doing? Something's Brewing!"

If a vulnerable pair bids too much it may be worthwhile to double. However, in a competitive auction, distribution is a key factor and a double may easily boomerang. Instead of visualizing the size of the vulnerable penalty, a player may well ask himself, "Why are the vulnerable opponents bidding so much?"

In today's hand, played in an important playoff match during the International Team Trials, West may well have asked this question.

North-South vulnerable
Dealer South

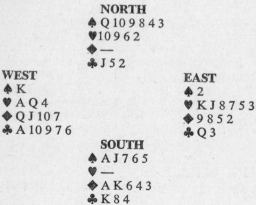

```
                    NORTH
                   ♠ Q 10 9 8 4 3
                   ♥ 10 9 6 2
                   ♦ —
                   ♣ J 5 2
      WEST                          EAST
     ♠ K                           ♠ 2
     ♥ A Q 4                       ♥ K J 8 7 5 3
     ♦ Q J 10 7                    ♦ 9 8 5 2
     ♣ A 10 9 7 6                  ♣ Q 3
                    SOUTH
                   ♠ A J 7 6 5
                   ♥ —
                   ♦ A K 6 4 3
                   ♣ K 8 4
```

The bidding:

South	West	North	East
1 ♠	Dbl.	3 ♠	4 ♥
4 ♠	Dbl.	All pass	

Opening lead: Queen of diamonds.

150

After West's takeout double, North made a barricade bid of three spades. In this situation the bid shows good trumps, good distribution, and few high cards. If North had the balance of power, he could have easily passed to await developments or chosen to redouble to assume captaincy. After East bid four hearts and South bid four spades, West faced his moment of decision.

He judged that his side had the majority of the high cards and he doubled. After all, East had bid and he was looking at quite a few face cards himself. How many spades could they make?

West was soon to find out. But he was not going to be happy with the news. The lead of the diamond queen was won by declarer, dummy discarding a club. Declarer cashed the spade ace, felling the king and drawing the opponents' trumps.

Declarer discarded another of dummy's clubs on the remaining high diamond and a low diamond was ruffed in dummy. A heart was ruffed by declarer and another diamond ruffed in dummy.

Declarer's fifth diamond was now established. A heart ruff placed declarer in his hand and dummy's last club was discarded on the long diamond. Declarer crossruffed clubs and hearts and took all thirteen tricks.

West's double turned out to be costly. Declarer scored 200 for each overtrick for a total of 1,390 points. The double cost about 700 points or 12 international match points.

Should West have doubled? Obviously, not on this hand. However, before doubling in these situations, two questions must be answered. Has South heard the bidding and has he noted the vulnerability? Who is South? It just doesn't pay to double some declarers.

One of these declarers is today's South, Sammy Kehela of Canada. He makes more than his share of doubled contracts.

DEFEATING DEFENSE
"The Ambassador Ducks the Trap—and Vice Versa"

The Italians know their way around the bridge table. Italy, represented by the unforgettable Blue Team, won twelve world titles to firmly establish this fact. Italy's permanent representative to the United Nations, Ambassador Piero Vinci, establishes another fact. Good play is not limited to Italy's top-echelon players.

Witness Vinci's defense of today's interesting game hand. Vinci held today's West cards.

Both vulnerable
Dealer South

```
                        NORTH
                        ♠ A J 8 5
                        ♥ A K
                        ♦ 7 5 3
                        ♣ A K J 10
        WEST                                EAST
        ♠ 3                                 ♠ Q 10 9
        ♥ J 10 7 4 3                        ♥ Q 8 5 2
        ♦ A Q                               ♦ K J 9 6
        ♣ 9 8 6 5 4                         ♣ 7 2
                        SOUTH
                        ♠ K 7 6 4 2
                        ♥ 9 6
                        ♦ 10 8 4 2
                        ♣ Q 3
```

The bidding:

South	West	North	East
Pass	Pass	1 ♣	Pass
1 ♠	Pass	4 ♠	All pass

Opening lead: Jack of hearts.

The bidding was over quickly. North lost no time in bidding game after South's one-spade response. North's hand evaluated to about 21 points in support of spades and, opposite a most skimpy response, a reasonable play for game was probable.

West led the heart jack won in the dummy with the king. Declarer then cashed the heart ace and two high spades to get the bad news. Declarer then started clubs, hoping to discard two of his losing diamonds, thereby holding his losses to two diamonds and one trump.

Examine the play if East makes a slight slip in the defense. If East does not ruff the third round of clubs, declarer discards a losing diamond and leads dummy's last club. Now whether East ruffs or not, declarer can discard another losing diamond to make his contract.

East made the winning play. He ruffed the third round of

clubs. However, the hand was not over yet. There was another trap to be avoided by the defense.

East made the obvious shift to diamonds and led the diamond 6. South followed with the deuce and Ambassador Vinci was at the crossroads.

Observe the results if he makes the obvious play of winning the queen. After cashing his diamond ace, Vinci would be forced to lead to dummy's high club or to make the equally disastrous lead of a heart for a ruff and discard.

The Ambassador avoided the trap. He properly analyzed that three diamond tricks were needed to beat the contract. Therefore, instead of blocking the diamond suit by winning cheaply with his queen, Vinci played his ace and then his queen. It was then a simple matter for East to overtake and for the defense to take three diamond tricks.

Excellent analysis by the defense—a result not unworthy of an Italian team.

SALVAGING THE PREEMPT
"Calling the Bidder's Bluff"

Bidding over a preempt is never a routine venture—even for top champions.

Today's hand was played in the 1971 world championship final between France and The Aces. It came in the second session when France was scoring heavily to reduce the margin The Aces had piled up in the first session.

Observe how differing actions taken over an opponent's preempt by Ace Bobby Goldman and Roger Trezel of France resulted in checking the French advance and swinging the momentum back in favor of The Aces.

Both vulnerable
Dealer North

NORTH
♠ 9 5 3 2
♥ 10 3
♦ K 7 3 2
♣ J 10 5

WEST
♠ A K Q J 4
♥ 6 4
♦ A Q 10
♣ K 9 4

EAST
♠ 10 8 7
♥ Q 2
♦ J 9 8 6
♣ 8 6 3 2

SOUTH
♠ 6
♥ A K J 9 8 7 5
♦ 5 4
♣ A Q 7

The bidding:

North	East	South	West
Pass	Pass	4 ♥	Dbl.
Pass	Pass	Pass	

When the hand was first played, Ace Bobby Wolff bid four hearts with the South hand. Roger Trezel decided to make a cooperative double with the West hand. Having no offensive potential, East, Dr. Pierre Jais of Paris, passed the double, resting all hope on the possibility that West had enough to defeat the contract.

Wolff had no trouble with his doubled contract. Fortunately for him, the hearts behaved nicely and the diamond king was well placed. Wolff lost only one spade, one diamond, and one club and scored 690 points.

When the hand was replayed, Henri Svarc of Paris also bid four hearts with the South hand. Ace Bobby Goldman chose a different course than his counterpart West, and, instead of doubling, he made the winning bid of four spades.

The defense scored two hearts, one diamond, and one club to beat the contract one trick—100 points for France. (The defense failed to find an early club shift and Goldman was able to discard a small club on a long diamond.)

The Aces scored 790 points in one room and lost 100 points in the other for a net gain of 690 points or 12 international match points.

Had the French defended with complete accuracy, the net

difference would have still been 590 points or 11 IMPs. A most welcome swing at an opportune moment when the French were battering at the gates.

THE SWINDLE PLAY
"Fighting the Unbeatable Foe—and Winning!"

Bobby Goldman of The Aces frequently answers to the name of "Mr. Percentage." This is because his coach and manager, Joe Musumeci, frequently asks him to compute the probabilities of various complex card combinations.

Since The Aces are graded on their selection of plays, Bobby's computations frequently aid in minimizing lengthy discussions arising out of differences of opinion.

By and large, The Aces stay with the percentages and avoid plays based upon a hunch or the swindle. However, every so often a hand comes along where even Mr. Percentage feels he must forsake the best technical play in favor of the swindle.

Observe Mr. Percentage in action on a hand played during one of The Aces' inter-squad training matches.

North-South vulnerable
Dealer North

```
                    NORTH
                    ♠ A 10 5
                    ♥ J 4
                    ♦ A J 10 7
                    ♣ A J 10 2
    WEST                              EAST
    ♠ K Q J 4                        ♠ 9 7 6 2
    ♥ 8                              ♥ Q 9 5
    ♦ K 9 8 6                        ♦ Q 4 3 2
    ♣ 9 7 5 4                        ♣ 8 3
                    Goldman
                    SOUTH
                    ♠ 8 3
                    ♥ A K 10 7 6 3 2
                    ♦ 5
                    ♣ K Q 6
```

The bidding:

North	East	South	West
1 NT	Pass	4 ♣*	Pass
4 NT**	Pass	5 ♣*	Pass
5 ♦***	Pass	6 ♥	Pass
Pass	Pass		

Opening lead: King of spades.

*Gerber convention
**Three aces
***No kings

North's opening bid of one no-trump was based upon only 15 high-card points. However, the possession of three aces and three 10s justified the bid.

Goldman's bid of four clubs was the Gerber convention, asking for aces. Goldman reasoned that his fine seven-card suit and side values should produce a slam unless his side was off two aces. Goldman settled for a small slam when he found out that North had no kings.

When dummy came down, it was obvious to Bobby that if he dropped the heart queen, thirteen tricks were available in top cards. However, after winning the spade ace and playing the two top trumps, the bad trump division gave Bobby a handful of problems.

At this stage you are asked to study all four hands and decide on the best sequence of plays to the next few tricks.

The percentage play is to try to establish a diamond trick in dummy by ruffing out K-Q-x of diamonds in either opponent's hand. If that fails, then the clubs could be run, hoping that at least three clubs can be cashed without a ruff in order to throw the losing spade on the fourth club.

The swindle play, which in Bobby's opinion offered a better chance of success than the percentage play, was to play the club suit as follows:

King of clubs at trick four and a low club to the ace. Now the jack of clubs from dummy. If East follows, it is all over. Bobby can return to dummy with the diamond ace and discard the losing spade on the fourth club.

However, if East is out of clubs, Bobby's deceptive play of the suit may induce East to believe that South is also out of clubs. If so, he may be afraid to ruff the jack, thinking that he will allow Bobby to discard a loser while he ruffed in.

East, in fact, did discard on the jack of clubs and "Mr. Percentage" made his slam. It's a good thing! Otherwise Bobby may have been answering to the name of "Mr. Hunch" rather than "Mr. Percentage."

CLOSE DOUBLES
"Why Not Spare the Wear and Tear?"

Close doubles of part-score contracts are avoided by all experienced players. Often the potential gain is not worth the risk involved and a slight miscalculation in defense can result in disaster. However, sometimes even the most experienced and wary player can be backed into a corner.

Today's hand, played by The Aces vs. Taiwan in the 1971 World Championship, vividly demonstrates this point. Witness the results of a close-penalty double of a part-score contract.

None vulnerable
Dealer North

                    NORTH
                    ♠ 10 9 8
                    ♥ Q 10
                    ♦ Q 8 5 2
                    ♣ Q 6 5 2

WEST   **EAST**
♠ 7 5 4 2   ♠ A J 3
♥ A J 8   ♥ 7 2
♦ A 7 4   ♦ K J 10 9
♣ J 10 3   ♣ A 8 7 4

                    SOUTH
                    ♠ K Q 6
                    ♥ K 9 6 5 4 3
                    ♦ 6 3
                    ♣ K 9

The bidding:

North	East	South	West
Pass	1 NT	2 ♥	Double
Pass	Pass	Pass	

Opening lead: Jack of clubs.

When the hand was first played with The Aces holding the East-West cards, East opened the bidding with one diamond and, after a one-heart overcall by South, West played at an unmolested one no-trump. When the Chinese held the East-West cards the bidding was as shown. Playing a weak no-trump (12-15 points), East's one no-trump forced South (Ace Bobby Goldman) one level higher if he chose to bid. Choose he did, and West (Stephen Chua) was faced with a murderous problem.

Consider the alternatives. Could he pass holding two aces and two jacks opposite an opening bid? Could he bid spades on that anemic "suit"? Two no-trump would be an overbid and might propel the partnership to a bad game. He didn't like the double; however, he liked the other choices less.

West led the club jack, ducked by dummy and East, and declarer won the king. Declarer led a low heart and guessed correctly, playing the 10. The spade 10 was led, East ducked and declarer allowed it to ride and held the trick. Declarer switched back to hearts and was able to scramble home with eight tricks losing only one spade, one heart, two diamonds, and one club.

Declarer was very lucky. The little he found in dummy was very useful and strategically placed.

During play (watched by a large excited audience), Tannah Hirsch, American Contract Bridge League representative, pointed out a defense to defeat the contract.

When declarer led the spade 10, East could rise with the ace to play a low diamond. Declarer would ruff the third round and lead hearts. West would then win the heart ace, put East on lead with the club ace, and a fourth diamond would promote West's trump jack to the setting trick.

Do you see why close doubles of part scores are avoided? It just isn't worth the wear and tear on the mind and body and the rapport of the partnership. For that matter, it doesn't help one's scores either!

ADVANTAGE TO OPENING BID . . . SOMETIMES
"Fate Has Some Surprises in Store"

The side which makes the opening bid usually enjoys a distinct advantage. So much so that most modern authorities have reduced the high card requirement for opening bids. However, there is always a hand which proves the exception.

Observe the unusual results of today's hand played in the qualifying rounds of the 1971 World Championships between The Aces and Australia.

North-South vulnerable
Dealer East

                        NORTH
                        ♠ 10 4 3 2
                        ♥ K 7 5
                        ♦ Q 10
                        ♣ A 10 7 4

        WEST   EAST
        ♠ 9 7   ♠ J 8
        ♥ J 6   ♥ A 9 3 2
        ♦ K 9 8 7 6 5   ♦ A J 4 3 2
        ♣ K Q 9   ♣ J 8

                        SOUTH
                        ♠ A K Q 6 5
                        ♥ Q 10 8 4
                        ♦ —
                        ♣ 6 5 3 2

The bidding:

East	South	West	North
1 ♥	1 ♠	Dbl.	3 ♠
Pass	4 ♠	All pass	

Opening lead: Jack of hearts.

When The Aces held the East-West cards, Bobby Wolff
opened the bidding with the East hand. Playing The Aces'
club, the light opening bids are routine and always made in a
four-card major suit, if possible. After South (Jim Borin)
overcalled one spade, West (Jim Jacoby) made a negative
double which promised a smattering of cards and support for
the unbid suits. North (Mrs. Borin) crowded the auction with
a jump to three spades, silencing East, and South carried on
to game.

After West led the heart jack there was little left to the play
and declarer lost only one heart and two clubs. The contract
was made and Australia scored 620 points for the vulnerable
game.

When the hand was replayed, the Australian East chose to
pass the East hand and the bidding went:

East	South	West	North
Pass	1 ♠	2 ♦	2 ♠
4 ♦	All pass		

This time Ace Mike Lawrence opened the bidding with the South cards. West (Dick Cummings) overcalled two diamonds and North (Bobby Goldman) bid two spades. East (Tim Seres), having passed originally, came to life with a leap to four diamonds, which ended the auction. West lost two spades, one heart, and one club for down one; 50 points to The Aces.

What an unusual twist of fate! The Aces opened the bidding at both tables, only to have the preemptive tactics of the Australians commandeer the auction in both rooms.

The Australians gained 620 points in one room and lost only 50 points in the other. A net gain of 570 points or 11 international match points.

Which proves that sometimes, even when you get your cake and eat it, too, it may leave a bad taste.

TIMING THE DEFENSE

"Skunk-Trapping Governor Sets His Goals, Then Quietly Pursues Them to a Colorful End"

Gov. Preston Smith of Texas has never had it easy. Restless and supercharged with energy, in his youth Governor Smith did everything from trapping skunks to fixing flats and pumping gas. About this skunk-trapping he says, "I was sprayed many a time and couldn't get in the house for a week. Nobody would have anything to do with me." Answering critical reporters who picture him as less than glamorous, he snaps back, "Colorless! Why, I'm the most colorful governor we ever had."

Governor Smith's social bridge group has often seen some of his color at the bridge table. He and his wife, Ima, have added spice and color to the same group for some thirty years. Witness their sparkling defense of today's hand. Governor Smith was East and Mrs. Smith sat West.

East-West vulnerable
Dealer North

NORTH
♠ Q J 7
♥ K Q 6 4
♦ K Q J 2
♣ A 7

WEST
♠ K 5
♥ 7 3
♦ 9 8 6 5
♣ Q J 9 4 3

EAST
♠ A 9 6 4 2
♥ A 8
♦ A 4
♣ 10 8 6 2

SOUTH
♠ 10 8 3
♥ J 10 9 5 2
♦ 10 7 3
♣ K 5

The bidding:

North	East	South	West
1 NT	Pass	2 ♥	All pass

Opening lead: King of spades.

South bought the contract for two hearts after North opened with a standard 16-18 point one no-trump.

Mrs. Smith found the inspired lead of the spade king. She deduced from the bidding that the governor was marked with high cards and a spade honor was just as likely as any other. Governor Smith played his 9 on the king, signaling for a continuation. However, after winning his spade ace, instead of giving Mrs. Smith an immediate ruff, he paused for some study.

He counted two spades and a ruff, the heart ace, and the diamond ace for five defensive tricks. Where was the other to come from?

He decided to leave nothing to chance, and instead of leading a spade for an immediate ruff, he led the ace and another diamond. Declarer won the diamond in dummy and tried to sneak off dummy with a small heart.

Governor Smith had his mind made up and he rose quickly with his trump ace. He now led a spade which Mrs. Smith ruffed for the fifth defensive trick. Mrs. Smith had no problem choosing a suit to lead for the setting trick. The governor's defense had made it clear that he could ruff a diamond. Down one.

It was excellent timing of the defense by Governor and Mrs. Smith. In the words of a long-time associate, "He is really not a complex man. He just sets his goals and moves in a straight line toward them."

EXTRA CARE IN SLAM PLAY
"Diplomatic Play on the Road to Morocco"

Hardly anyone expects an ambassador to play top-level bridge. However, bridge players in the Washington, D.C., area had several opportunities at a recent regional tournament to watch former Moroccan ambassador to the United States, Ahmed Osman.

Witness the excellent play of today's slam hand by Osman, who sat South.

None vulnerable
Dealer South

```
                    NORTH
                    ♠ J 10 8 7 6
                    ♥ A 4 3
                    ♦ J 4
                    ♣ K 7 6
  WEST                                    EAST
  ♠ Q 3                                   ♠ K 9 5 4 2
  ♥ K Q J 9 7 6                           ♥ 10 8
  ♦ 10 5 2                                ♦ 9 8
  ♣ 10 5                                  ♣ J 9 8 3
                    SOUTH
                    ♠ A
                    ♥ 5 2
                    ♦ A K Q 7 6 3
                    ♣ A Q 4 2
```

The bidding:

South	West	North	East
1 ♦	1 ♥	1 ♠	Pass
3 ♣	Pass	3 ♥	Pass
4 ♦	Pass	5 ♦	Pass
6 ♦	Pass	Pass	Pass

Opening lead: King of hearts.

Although the bidding was aggressive, the final contract was certainly reasonable.

Note that many modern players would prefer to make a weak jump overcall of two hearts instead of a regular overcall of one heart with the West hand. Over South's jump shift, North cue bid the heart ace and Ambassador Osman was on his way to his slam.

The simple play for the slam is to draw trumps, concede a heart trick and pray for the club suit to divide evenly. Alternate plays of drawing only one trump, and ruffing the fourth club with the diamond jack if clubs fail to divide, are too far-fetched.

As the reader can see, either approach would lead to defeat. However, Osman found the winning line of play.

The heart ace was won in dummy and a spade was led to declarer's ace. A low diamond was played to dummy's jack and a low spade was ruffed by declarer. This dropped an honor from West and placed the burden of protecting the spade suit with East.

Trumps were drawn and a heart trick conceded. West won the heart and continued with another, which declarer ruffed. The ambassador next played all his trumps but one to produce this position:

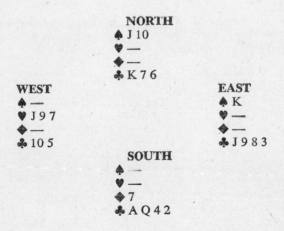

NORTH
♠ J 10
♥ —
♦ —
♣ K 7 6

WEST
♠ —
♥ J 9 7
♦ —
♣ 10 5

EAST
♠ K
♥ —
♦ —
♣ J 9 8 3

SOUTH
♠ —
♥ —
♦ 7
♣ A Q 4 2

On the lead of the last trump, the ambassador discarded dummy's 10 of spades and East had an impossible discard. If he threw the spade king, dummy's jack would be high; if he discarded a club, the ambassador's clubs would be established.

A well-played hand and well-deserved slam. Osman took a little extra care in catering to a favorable lie of the cards in the spade suit in case clubs did not split. This extra care resulted in success of the contract, a reward that was well deserved.

CARD LOCATION BY DEDUCTION
"Two-Fisted Finessing by Jimmy"

Jimmy Stewart leads an unusually active life. One of the greatest stars of the movie industry who starred in "Fool's Parade," he has won an Oscar for the best actor of the year and has had five other Oscar nominations. He retired from the U. S. Air Force Reserve as a brigadier general, is a trustee of Claremont College, California, and a member of the executive board of the Los Angeles Council of the Boy Scouts of America.

Jimmy Stewart also finds time to play a good game of bridge. Witness his analysis in the play of today's game contract. He held today's South cards.

East-West vulnerable
Dealer West

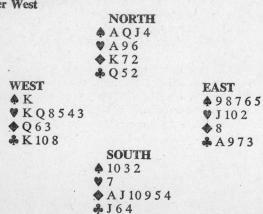

```
                    NORTH
                    ♠ A Q J 4
                    ♥ A 9 6
                    ♦ K 7 2
                    ♣ Q 5 2
    WEST                              EAST
    ♠ K                              ♠ 9 8 7 6 5
    ♥ K Q 8 5 4 3                    ♥ J 10 2
    ♦ Q 6 3                          ♦ 8
    ♣ K 10 8                         ♣ A 9 7 3
                    SOUTH
                    ♠ 10 3 2
                    ♥ 7
                    ♦ A J 10 9 5 4
                    ♣ J 6 4
```

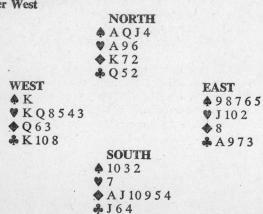

The bidding:

West	North	East	South
1 ♥	Dbl.	2 ♥	3 ♦
Pass	3 ♥	Pass	4 ♥
Pass	5 ♦	Pass	Pass
Pass			

Opening lead: King of hearts.

East's raise over North's double probably helped North-South reach the five-diamond game. After Stewart entered the bidding voluntarily at the three level, North cue-bid three hearts to invite game. Stewart was quick to accept with a cue bid of his own, and North bid five diamonds.

Against West's lead of the heart king, Stewart found the winning line of play. He won the ace of hearts in dummy and led a low diamond to his ace.

The jack of diamonds followed, finessed successfully. West's diamond queen was picked up, and Stewart trumped a heart to return to his hand.

A low spade to dummy fetched West's king, captured by dummy's ace. The spades were all high and Stewart was able to discard one of his clubs on dummy's fourth spade. He was left with only two club losers and made eleven tricks and his contract.

Was Stewart clairvoyant, or had he peeked in somebody's hand? Neither. He analyzed the situation correctly.

He deduced that the ace and king of clubs were not in West's hand, since the chances were good that West would have chosen to lead the club king from a holding of A-K. From this analysis, he knew that if he played the clubs himself he would have to lose three club tricks. Therefore, he had to find a favorable situation in spades to provide for a club discard.

What about the finesse of the diamond queen? This play was not luck either. Since West was presumed to have started with only one club honor, Stewart decided to play West for the diamond queen to justify his opening bid.

Excellent analysis and confident execution by Stewart brought home the contract. A typical Jimmy Stewart performance.

AGGRESSIVE BIDDING
"Bid 'Em High? Or Pass with Class?"

Aggressive bidding and play is the hallmark of many top players. This school believes that "bidding full value" whenever a reasonable excuse exists is preferable to a pass. Most often, these players produce results that substantiate their convictions. However, sometimes fate can take an unusual turn.

Today's hand was played in the qualifying rounds of the 1971 World Championship between France and The Aces. Witness the unusual results achieved by players choosing divergent courses.

None vulnerable
Dealer East

```
                        NORTH
                        ♠ 10 3 2
                        ♥ K 9 3
                        ♦ A K 9 5
                        ♣ K J 7
        WEST                            EAST
        ♠ A K 8 7 5                     ♠ J 9 6
        ♥ A J 7                         ♥ 10 6 5 2
        ♦ J 4 3                         ♦ Q 10 8 6
        ♣ Q 6                           ♣ 10 3
                        SOUTH
                        ♠ Q 4
                        ♥ Q 8 4
                        ♦ 7 2
                        ♣ A 9 8 5 4 2
```

The bidding:

East	South	West	North
Pass	Pass	1 ♠	Dbl.
Pass	3 ♣	All pass	

Opening lead: Ace of spades

When the hand was first played, with Aces Jim Jacoby and Bobby Wolff holding the North-South cards, this aggressive pair reached a contract of three clubs after Jim Jacoby (North) made a takeout double of one spade. An aggressive bidder like Jacoby would look for a hiding place if he ever passed with the North hand.

However, aggressiveness doesn't always lead to aggressive contracts. Over Wolff's three-club response, an invitational bid showing 8-11 points, Jacoby visualized no games and passed. A most reasonable choice. Wolff played a tranquil part score and made an overtrick for a score of 130 points.

In the other room the French North (Henri Svarc) chose the conservative pass over one spade. The bidding:

East	South	West	North
Pass	Pass	1 ♠	Pass
Pass	2 ♣	Pass	2 ♠
Pass	2 NT	Pass	3 NT
All pass			

Opening lead: Seven of spades.

After failing to bid at his first turn, North compensated with aggressiveness at his second turn. After South reopened with two clubs, North first cue-bid the spade suit and then raised to the no-trump game.

West led his fourth-best spade, which was won by South's queen. The fortunate drop of the club queen quickly inflated declarer's trick total to nine—six clubs, two diamonds and one spade. Three no-trump bid and made.

An unusual turn of events. The aggressive player chooses an aggressive bid and reaches a nonaggressive, though sound, contract. The conservative player takes a conservative course only to reach an eventual aggressive contract requiring some lucky breaks.

Which is why bridge will always be a fascinating game. There are few dull moments.

SLAM PLAY
"Dandy Don Dupes the Dudes"

In his days as the fiery leader of the Dallas Cowboys, Don Meredith guided the most explosive offense in football. Few opposing teams contained the Cowboys' varied offensive alignments as Meredith quarterbacked an expansion club into an NFL power. Now he is a TV broadcaster on the Monday night pro football series.

Meredith is also familiar with innovative plays at the bridge table. Witness his play of today's fascinating slam contract. Meredith held today's South cards.

Both vulnerable
Dealer South

NORTH
♠ A Q 5
♥ 7 5 3
♦ Q 7 6
♣ A 10 7 4

WEST
♠ 4 2
♥ 10 9 8 6 2
♦ J 9 5 4 2
♣ 2

EAST
♠ 10 9 7 6 3
♥ A 4
♦ 10 8
♣ J 9 6 3

SOUTH
♠ K J 8
♥ K Q J
♦ A K 3
♣ K Q 8 5

The bidding:

South	West	North	East
2 NT	Pass	6 NT	All pass

Opening lead: Ten of hearts.

Meredith opened a standard two no-trump and North, knowing the combined hands had at least 32 points, bid the small slam.

West led the 10 of hearts which was won by East's ace. A heart return was won by South's queen.

Before Meredith called the next play, he took time out for a count of tricks. Three spades, two hearts, and three diamonds totalled eight tricks; he needed four more in clubs. With this club holding four tricks seemed easy, unless. . . .

Meredith cashed his last high heart and noted that West originally started with five hearts. Three top diamonds came next and West was discovered to have started with ten red cards.

Meredith was now in complete control. He had read his defenses beautifully and was in position to claim the contract. He knew West started with only three black cards. If two of them were clubs, four club winners were automatic. However, if West had only one club, a special play was necessary.

To determine West's spade holding, Meredith cashed his spade king and led another to dummy's queen. When West followed to both spades, he was marked with only one club.

Meredith cashed the club ace and led the club 10. When East refused to cover, Meredith let it ride, and scored his contract (if East had covered, Meredith would have reentered dummy with a small spade to the ace to finesse against East's 9).

Excellent planning and play by Don Meredith. He brushes off compliments says, "Shucks, that wasn't tough. That's one of the first things a quarterback has to learn—getting the count straight."

A GUESS IN THE BIDDING
"To Bid or Not to Bid"

Shortly after the 1970 world championship matches in Stockholm, Bobby Wolff of The Aces was asked, "Is there any particular hand that sticks in your mind?"

"There sure is," he replied, and he proceeded to amplify as follows:

"Much of the time bridge is a delightful game for me. Only one right play or bid exists, and my only problem is to find it. I enjoyed this feeling even during the world championship, although the pressure was intense.

"There are times, however, when bridge ceases to be delightful. Suddenly a problem is thrust upon you for which no right answer exists. There you sit, naked and defenseless. You must make a decision, and you know that the chances are good that you will look idiotic when the hand is over.

"Imagine being confronted with this sort of problem in a world championship with the eyes of the entire world of bridge looking over your shoulder!

"In our first qualifying match against Norway, I held the following hand:

♠ A K 9
♥ K 4
♦ A K Q 8 5 4
♣ 6 5

"Naturally, we were vulnerable and the opponents were not. My left-hand opponent opened the bidding with three clubs, my partner bid three spades, and my right-hand opponent bid five clubs! What would you do with that crate of ripe tomatoes?

"I squirmed, I coughed, I asked for some ice water. To no avail. It was still my turn to bid.

"How many club losers does partner have? Might he be void? Are spades the right trump suit or might diamonds be better? Where on earth do I find the answer to this one?

"Finally I decided this decision was too much for one person and I bid six clubs. This would get Jim Jacoby in the picture and he might be in a position to clarify things. Besides, it was only right that he be allowed to share in whatever rewards lay in store for us.

"Jim bid six spades over six clubs and I passed gratefully. And apprehensively."

The entire deal was:

North-South vulnerable
Dealer West

```
                    NORTH
                 ♠ Q J 10 7 6 2
                 ♥ A Q 8 7 5
                 ♦ —
                 ♣ J 7
   WEST                              EAST
 ♠ 8 5                             ♠ 4 3
 ♥ 6 2                             ♥ J 10 9 3
 ♦ 10 9 2                          ♦ J 7 6 3
 ♣ K Q 10 9 8 4                    ♣ A 3 2
                    SOUTH
                 ♠ A K 9
                 ♥ K 4
                 ♦ A K Q 8 5 4
                 ♣ 6 5
```

The bidding:

Larsen	Jacoby	Koppang	Wolff
West	**North**	**East**	**South**
3 ♣	3 ♠	5 ♣	6 ♣
Pass	6 ♠	Pass	Pass
Pass			

Opening lead: Ace of clubs.

"My nightmare had come alive as the defense cashed two quick club tricks to defeat the contract. I was certain that I had kicked 13 IMPs under the table. How can I ever forget this one?"

When the hand was replayed at the other table, Bobby

Goldman and Billy Eisenberg did nothing to simplify things for their opponents.

Goldman also opened the bidding with three clubs. North cue-bid four clubs, anticipating a four-level major suit response that he would pass. However, Eisenberg raised to five clubs.

This placed Wolff's Norwegian counterpart in an even worse position. He had reason to believe his partner held a stronger hand. His guess was seven diamonds, which was defeated three tricks. A five IMP gain for The Aces!

In retrospect, we might conclude that some mighty poor decisions were made. Might we be thinking otherwise if North's diamond and club holding had been interchanged? Anyway, it's good to see that even our superstars have to guess once in awhile!

USE ALL THE CHANCES
"Two to One Beats Even Money at My Bookmaker's"

Earlier this year several Aces traveled with me to visit the Everglades Club in Palm Beach. There, three of us had the pleasure of playing with the wife of "Mr. Palm Beach," Mrs. Charles Munn. I might add that Mrs. Munn took The Aces in stride, and finished on the plus side of the ledger.

Observe how Mrs. Munn played today's slam hand to add to our point total. Our opponents were Aces Jim Jacoby and Bob Hamman.

North-South vulnerable
Dealer South

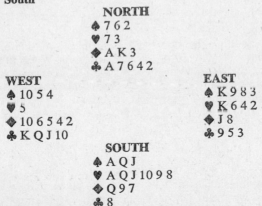

```
                    NORTH
                    ♠ 7 6 2
                    ♥ 7 3
                    ♦ A K 3
                    ♣ A 7 6 4 2
    WEST                              EAST
    ♠ 10 5 4                         ♠ K 9 8 3
    ♥ 5                              ♥ K 6 4 2
    ♦ 10 6 5 4 2                     ♦ J 8
    ♣ K Q J 10                       ♣ 9 5 3
                    SOUTH
                    ♠ A Q J
                    ♥ A Q J 10 9 8
                    ♦ Q 9 7
                    ♣ 8
```

The bidding:

South	West	North	East
1 ♥	Pass	2 ♣	Pass
3 ♥	Pass	4 ♦	Pass
4 ♠	Pass	4 NT	Pass
5 ♥	Pass	6 ♥	Pass
Pass	Pass		

Opening lead: King of clubs.

The slam was well bid and a good contract. Over my two-club bid, Mrs. Munn jumped in hearts, and over my cue bid of four diamonds, she cue-bid four spades. It was then easy for me to ask for aces and bid the slam. All that remained was for Mrs. Munn to bring it home.

All is not as easy as it seems, even though both the spade king and the heart king are finessable. Witness what a bit of carelessness will do.

Declarer wins the club king with dummy's ace and finesses in trumps. All appears well, since the finesse works. Declarer returns to dummy with a high diamond and repeats the trump finesse. This works again.

However, after West discards, it becomes obvious that East's king of trumps cannot be captured. The only hope left for declarer is to avoid the loss of a spade trick.

Declarer returns to dummy with the remaining high diamond and tries the spade finesse. This works also, but when the spade ace fails to capture the spade king, declarer goes down to defeat.

How did Mrs. Munn make the hand? By careful planning of her use of dummy's entries.

After winning the opening lead with the club ace, Mrs. Munn finessed a spade rather than a trump. When this held the trick, she returned to dummy to repeat the spade finesse. Since Mrs. Munn had no spade losers, she was more than happy to surrender a heart trick.

And what if West had won the first spade finesse? Then Mrs. Munn could fall back on the heart finesse, using dummy's ace and king of diamonds to take two finesses. Declarer had nothing to lose, since the delayed heart finesse would have succeeded whenever the immediate heart finesse did.

Something similar to: "Two shots are better than one." Or, "You can have your cake and eat it, too."

172

EXPERTISE AD ABSURDUM
"If You've Got a Reason That Rhymes—Don't Think"

One of S. J. Simon's immortal characters was the "Unlucky Expert." The Unlucky Expert was a thoroughly developed bridge technician. His bidding and play were beyond reproach and his analyses always correct.

His only problem was that he was a purist and never could make allowances for the shortcomings of his partner, nor for the aberrations of his opponents.

Observe how an advanced analysis of today's game hand led declarer to his downfall.

Both vulnerable
Dealer North

```
                    NORTH
                    ♠ A K 3
                    ♥ 9
                    ♦ 10 5
                    ♣ K J 8 7 6 3 2
   WEST                              EAST
   ♠ 7 4                            ♠ J 10 9 5
   ♥ K 7 6 4 2                      ♥ J 10 8 3
   ♦ K Q 9 6                        ♦ A 7 3
   ♣ 10 4                           ♣ Q 9
                    SOUTH
                    ♠ Q 8 6 2
                    ♥ A Q 5
                    ♦ J 8 4 2
                    ♣ A 5
```

The bidding:

North	East	South	West
1 ♣	Pass	1 ♠	Pass
2 ♠	Pass	3 NT	Pass
Pass	Pass		Pass

Opening lead: King of diamonds.

Over South's response of one spade, North had a choice. He could rebid his seven-card club suit or he could raise to two spades. He chose the latter, not wishing to hide his fine spade holding.

Over North's raise, South leaped directly to a no-trump

173

game. This bid denied a five-card spade suit and asked North to pass unless he held four-card trump support.

With the lead of the diamond king and diamond continuation, the defense took the first four tricks.

After winning West's exit, any declarer except the Unlucky Expert would make the contract by playing the A-K of clubs, dropping East's queen. The cliché of "eight ever, nine never" would be applied religiously and the hand filed away and forgotten.

Not so with the Unlucky Expert. He always finds a technically correct reason for making the losing play. Observe.

After the play of the first four diamonds, West exited with a spade. The Unlucky Expert won in dummy and cashed two more rounds of spades.

When West discarded on the third spade, the Unlucky Expert knew West had started with seven cards in clubs and hearts. This was not enough to steer him astray, so he reasoned further. West could not have more than four hearts or he certainly would have led hearts instead of diamonds. Ergo! West must have at least three clubs, and East, at most, a singleton.

The Unlucky Expert played his ace of clubs and confidently followed with a finesse of dummy's jack. East won his queen, cashed a high spade and then led the heart jack. Down four.

A result worthy of only the Unlucky Expert.

THESE TWO QUIZ HANDS WERE TAKEN FROM a match involving both North American teams who have earned the right to play in the 1971 world championships.

The Aces participated as the defending 1970 champions. Four Los Angeles players, Lew Mathe, Don Krauss, Richard Walsh and John Swanson, and two easterners, Edgar Kaplan of New York City and Norman Kay of Philadelphia, won the right to be the other team.

Question No. 1. You are South, all vulnerable, and hold:

> ♠ K 10 9 8 6 3
> ♥ 8 7 4 3
> ♦ —
> ♣ 9 6 5

The bidding:

South	West	North	East
Pass	1 NT	Pass	Pass
?			

Do you bid two spades or do you pass?

Question No. 2. You are South, North-South vulnerable, and hold:

> ♠ A 9 6 5
> ♥ Q 10 7 5 3
> ♦ A Q 6
> ♣ 4

The bidding:

South	West	North	East
1 ♥	4 ♣	4 ♥	Pass
Pass	5 ♣	Pass	Pass
?			

Answer No. 1. If you bid two spades, you lose 9 IMPs. Pass, and you may break even. The entire hand:

All vulnerable
Dealer South

Hamman
NORTH
♠ A 5
♥ K 9 5
♦ A K 9 3
♣ Q 10 8 2

Krauss
WEST
♠ Q 7 4
♥ A Q J
♦ Q J 10 5 2
♣ A 7

Mathe
EAST
♠ J 2
♥ 10 6 2
♦ 8 7 6 4
♣ K J 4 3

Lawrence
SOUTH
♠ K 10 9 8 6 3
♥ 8 7 4 3
♦ —
♣ 9 6 5

Ace Mike Lawrence decided to bid two spades when Krauss's bid of one no-trump was passed to him. Bob Hamman, who doesn't enjoy passing, could restrain himself no longer and jumped to game. Four spades was down one.

At the other table, Walsh elected to pass, and one no-trump was defeated three tricks after declarer went wrong in the play.

Answer No. 2. Double loses five IMPs; pass loses 11 IMPs; five hearts breaks even, six hearts gains 13 IMPs. The entire hand:

North-South vulnerable
Dealer South

Walsh
NORTH
♠ K Q 10 7
♥ A K 9 4
♦ K 9 2
♣ 7 2

Lawrence
WEST
♠ J 4 2
♥ 2
♦ 7
♣ A K Q J 10 8 6 3

Hamman
EAST
♠ 8 3
♥ J 8 6
♦ J 10 8 5 4 3
♣ 9 5

Swanson
SOUTH
♠ A 9 6 5
♥ Q 10 7 5 3
♦ A Q 6
♣ 4

Swanson elected to double five clubs. Lawrence went down three tricks, the defense limiting him to his solid club winners.

At the other table, Aces Jim Jacoby and Bob Wolff played a five-heart contract after a jump to five clubs by West.

This is a very difficult hand to bid after the high preempt by West. North is robbed of all bidding space and is restrained by his doubleton club. South cannot know of all North's goodies and finds it difficult to bid further in spite of the singleton club.

THE FOLLOWING TWO EXCITING HANDS WERE played in the last Spingold tournament between North America's two international teams. Match wits and bids with them to see if you can better their results.

The Aces played to defend their 1970 world title in Taipei, Taiwan. Our second entry was a team of four Los Angeles players, Lew Mathe, Don Krauss, Richard Walsh and John Swanson, augmented by Edgar Kaplan of New York and Norman Kay of Philadelphia.

Question No. 1. You are South with none vulnerable and hold:

♠ J87532
♥ 4
♦ —
♣ J98632

You will play a special convention used by Aces Jim Jacoby and Bobby Wolff to show a very weak and highly distributional hand. An immediate cue bid of the opponent's heart opening shows two black suits.

The bidding:

East	South	West	North
1 ♥	2 ♥	3 ♣	5 ♣
Dbl.	Pass	5 ♠	Pass
6 ♦	?		

What do you bid?

Question No. 2. You are South, all vulnerable, and hold:

♠ J75
♥ KQ972
♦ 109
♣ K82

The bidding:

North	East	South	West
1 ♠	4 ♦	?	

What is your bid?

Answer No. 1. A sacrifice to seven clubs is the winner and gains 12 IMPs. Jacoby made the correct decision, was doubled and held his losses to 500 points (down three).

At the other table, Aces Bob Hamman and Mike Lawrence were doubled in six hearts, making, for a score of 1,210 points. The entire hand:

178

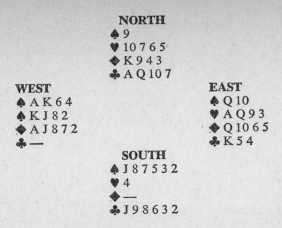

NORTH
♠ 9
♥ 10 7 6 5
♦ K 9 4 3
♣ A Q 10 7

WEST
♠ A K 6 4
♠ K J 8 2
♦ A J 8 7 2
♣ —

EAST
♠ Q 10
♥ A Q 9 3
♦ Q 10 6 5
♣ K 5 4

SOUTH
♠ J 8 7 5 3 2
♥ 4
♦ —
♣ J 9 8 6 3 2

Answer No. 2. If you bid four spades, you lose 8 IMPs. This will be doubled and defeated two tricks for 500 points. In the match, Walsh refused to be shut out and was punished.

At the other table, with the same bidding, Jim Jacoby decided to pass and avoid the penalty. Perhaps his system should be credited. In the Orange Club system, North's hand was limited to less than 17 high-card points and might contain only a four-card suit. Walsh's partner had promised a five card suit.

The entire hand:

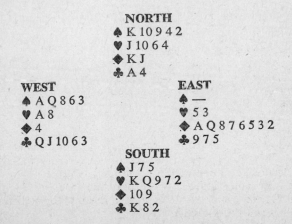

NORTH
♠ K 10 9 4 2
♥ J 10 6 4
♦ K J
♣ A 4

WEST
♠ A Q 8 6 3
♥ A 8
♦ 4
♣ Q J 10 6 3

EAST
♠ —
♥ 5 3
♦ A Q 8 7 6 5 3 2
♣ 9 7 5

SOUTH
♠ J 7 5
♥ K Q 9 7 2
♦ 10 9
♣ K 8 2

THIS QUIZ WILL TEST YOUR PLAY AND DEFENSE. The problems were taken from actual play situations encountered by The Aces. See if you can play as well or better.

Question No. 1. You are South and declarer at three no-trump. Plan your play (International Match Point or rubber bridge.).

NORTH
♠ K 3 2
♥ 4 3 2
♦ K 7
♣ A J 10 9 8

SOUTH
♠ A 8 7
♥ K 5
♦ A Q 4 3
♣ Q 7 6 5

South	West	North	East
1 ♦	1 ♠	2 ♣	Pass
2 NT	Pass	3 NT	Pass
Pass	Pass		

Opening lead: Queen of spades.

Question No. 2. You are East, defending three no-trump by South. The bidding:

South	West	North	East
	Pass	1 ♦	1 ♠
2 NT	Pass	3 NT	Pass
Pass			

Opening lead: Two of spades.

You win the ace and declarer plays the 7. How do you defend?

Dummy	You
NORTH	**EAST**
♠ 10 8 5	♠ A J 9 6 4
♥ 8 4	♥ K J 9
♦ A K 8 7 6 5	♦ 10
♣ K 6	♣ 10 9 5 4

Answer No. 1. Your should win the spade and play the ace of clubs. Take 10 IMPs if you refused to take the club finesse, as did Ace Billy Eisenberg when he played the hand in a recent practice match.

The entire hand:

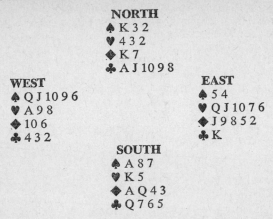

NORTH
♠ K 3 2
♥ 4 3 2
♦ K 7
♣ A J 10 9 8

WEST
♠ Q J 10 9 6
♥ A 9 8
♦ 10 6
♣ 4 3 2

EAST
♠ 5 4
♥ Q J 10 7 6
♦ J 9 8 5 2
♣ K

SOUTH
♠ A 8 7
♥ K 5
♦ A Q 4 3
♣ Q 7 6 5

South must refuse the club finesse because he can afford to lose a club trick to West, but not to East because of his vulnerable heart holding. Ducking one round of spades is not correct, since the opponents can switch to hearts before you establish clubs (in the event the club king did not drop).

Answer No. 2. If you win the spade ace and fail to shift to hearts, you lose seven IMPs. Ace Billy Eisenberg returned a spade after declarer's false card of the spade 7 playing his partner for the Q-3-2 of spades.

The entire hand:

NORTH
♠ 10 8 5
♥ 8 4
♦ A K 8 7 6 5
♣ K 6

WEST
♠ 2
♥ A Q 10 5
♦ 9 4 3 2
♣ Q 8 7 2

EAST
♠ A J 9 6 4
♥ K J 9
♦ 10
♣ 10 9 5 4

SOUTH
♠ K Q 7 3
♥ 7 6 3 2
♦ Q J
♣ A J 3

At the other table, your partners played a peaceful contract of three diamonds and made four. If you found the right defense, you would have gained 5 IMPs instead of losing 7 IMPs.

THESE QUIZ HANDS WERE PLAYED IN THE world's first exhibition match for mass audiences.

Sponsored by the *New Orleans Times-Picayune* and Crippled Children's Hospital earlier this year, the match pitted The Aces against a group of challengers from New Orleans. An average of one thousand spectators per session watched the four sessions of play.

Question No. 1. You are South, East-West vulnerable, and hold:

♠ J 9 7 5 3
♥ 7 3
♦ A 8 3 2
♣ Q 7

Do you continue to game after this bidding?

South	West	North	East
Pass	Pass	1 ♥	Pass
1 ♠	Pass	3 ♠	Pass
?			

Question No. 2. You are South, no vulnerability, and you hold:

♠ A K 6
♥ 10 3
♦ 8 6 4 2
♣ A 8 6 4

Do you continue on to game after: (three hearts is nonforcing)

East	South	West	North
Pass	1 ♣	Pass	1 ♥
Pass	1 NT	Pass	3 ♥
Pass	?		

Answer No. 1. If you pass, you lose 6 IMPs; if you continue to game, you break even. In the match, both pairs bid to game and there was no swing. The entire hand:

NORTH
- ♠ A K 6 4
- ♥ A K J 6 2
- ♦ 10 5
- ♣ 10 3

WEST
- ♠ Q 10
- ♥ Q 9 5 4
- ♦ Q 7 4
- ♣ A J 6 2

EAST
- ♠ 8 2
- ♥ 10 8
- ♦ K J 9 6
- ♣ K 9 8 5 4

SOUTH
- ♠ J 9 7 5 3
- ♥ 7 3
- ♦ A 8 3 2
- ♣ Q 7

Aces Billy Eisenberg and Bob Hamman played a two-diamond opening to show four spades and five hearts and 12-16 points (Flannery convention). Over two diamonds, Eisenberg leaped directly to the spade game.

In the other room, Julius Rosenblum, president of the World Bridge Federation, and Lou Gurvich had no trouble reaching game. North relieved South of any problems by leaping to four spades over the one-spade response.

Answer No. 2. If you continue on to game, as did Julius Rosenblum, you gain 6 IMPs. Game is on and was missed by The Aces in the other room.

The entire hand:

NORTH
- ♠ 10 7
- ♥ A J 9 8 6 5
- ♦ A
- ♣ Q 10 9 7

WEST
- ♠ 9 4 3 2
- ♥ K 4 2
- ♦ K 10 5 3
- ♣ J 2

EAST
- ♠ Q J 8 5
- ♥ Q 7
- ♦ Q J 9 7
- ♣ K 5 3

SOUTH
- ♠ A K 6
- ♥ 10 3
- ♦ 8 6 4 2
- ♣ A 8 6 4

On the combined holding, four hearts is a good game and eleven tricks were made by both declarers.

IN THE RECENT NATIONAL KNOCKOUT championship tournament for the Vanderbilt Cup, The Aces survived a thrilling match against another predominantly Texas team in the quarter-final round.

The Aces won by only 4 international match points, the match being decided by the last hand in play. The Aces' opponents were George Rosencranz of Mexico, John Gerber, Paul Hodge, G. R. Nail and Dan Morse of Houston, and Mark Blumenthal of Philadelphia.

Today's quiz is taken from hands played in this match. Compare your answers with those of the players.

Question No. 1. You are South, none vlunerable and hold:

♠ J 6 4 3
♥ A J 10 8 7 4 2
♦ —
♣ A 5

What do you bid in this situation?

South	West	North	East
1 ♥	Dbl.	Pass	2 ♦
2 ♥	Dbl.	Pass	3 NT
?			

Question No. 2. You are South, vulnerable, and hold:

♠ J 7 3
♥ K 8 5
♦ Q J 6 4
♣ K 6 2

What do you bid at this point?

West	North	East	South
3 ♣	3 ♥	4 ♣	?

Answer No. 1. If you bid four hearts as a sacrifice, it turns out to be a "phantom" sacrifice, since no games are on for the opponents. If you pass, you will easily defeat three no-trump with a heart lead. If the opponents reach a minor-suit game, it will also go down. The entire hand:

184

```
              NORTH
              ♠ 10 9 2
              ♥ Q 6
              ♦ K 8 7 4 2
              ♣ 10 9 4
WEST                        EAST
♠ A K Q 8                   ♠ 7 5
♥ 9 3                       ♥ K 5
♦ A 3                       ♦ Q J 10 9 6 5
♣ K Q 7 6 3                 ♣ J 8 2
              SOUTH
              ♠ J 6 4 3
              ♥ A J 10 8 7 4 2
              ♦ —
              ♣ A 5
```

In the match, The Aces gained 400 points or 9 IMPs. In one room, Aces Billy Eisenberg and Bob Hamman doubled South in four hearts and beat it two tricks (300). In the other room, Aces Mike Lawrence and Bobby Goldman defeated a doubled East-West five diamond contract one trick (100).

Answer No. 2. If you pass, you beat four clubs two tricks, but you also lose 520 points (11 IMPs). If you bid four hearts, you break even. The entire hand:

```
              NORTH
              ♠ K Q 9
              ♥ A 9 7 6 3
              ♦ A 10 3 2
              ♣ J
WEST                        EAST
♠ 8 5                       ♠ A 10 6 4 2
♥ J 10                      ♥ Q 4 2
♦ K 9 5                     ♦ 8 7
♣ A Q 10 9 7 3             ♣ 8 5 4
              SOUTH
              ♠ J 7 3
              ♥ K 8 5
              ♦ Q J 6 4
              ♣ K 6 2
```

In the match, Aces Eisenberg and Hamman were allowed to play in four clubs, while in the other room, Aces Lawrence and Goldman reached the four-heart contract, 11 more IMPs for The Aces.

The winning margin was only 4 IMPs. If the Rosencranz team had made the winning decision on either of these hands, The Aces would have lost the match and the tournament. How did you do?

THE NEXT QUIZ IS BASED ON HANDS PLAYED by The Aces in an important challenge match in Dallas. The opponents were Peter Pender and Grant Baze of San Francisco and Armand Barfus and Robert Rothlein of Miami.

Match your actions with those taken at the table.

Question No. 1. You are South, first hand of the long match, no vulnerability and hold:

> ♠ 6
> ♥ Q J 10
> ♦ A Q 8 7 6 5 4 3
> ♣ 4

You are the dealer. What is your bid?

Question No. 2. You are South, vulnerable vs. nonvulnerable, and hold:

> ♠ K
> ♥ A 4 2
> ♦ A Q 6
> ♣ K 10 9 6 5 4

What is your bid after this sequence?

West	North	East	South
3 ♠	Pass	4 ♠	?

Answer No. 1. If you preempted with three or four diamonds, you missed an easy heart game and lost 360 points on the deal. The entire hand:

                    NORTH
                    ♠ 10 9 5 4
                    ♥ A K 9 8 6 4
                    ♦ K
                    ♣ K 5

WEST   EAST
♠ A J 3   ♠ K Q 8 7 2
♥ 5   ♥ 7 3 2
♦ J 9 2   ♦ 10
♣ A J 9 7 6 3   ♣ Q 10 8 2

                    SOUTH
                    ♠ 6
                    ♥ Q J 10
                    ♦ A Q 8 7 6 5 4 3
                    ♣ 4

In the match, Peter Pender decided to start the fireworks
early and preempted with four diamonds. This was passed out
and Pender made five.

At the other table, Aces Jim Jacoby and Bobby Wolff rejected the preempt and had no trouble reaching the easy heart
game. The Aces gained 360 points or 8 international match
points on the deal.

Answer No. 2. If you pass, the opponents will score the
game for a large loss. If you choose the risky course and either double or bid five clubs, you will probably reach and
make a minor-suit game contract. The entire hand:

                    NORTH
                    ♠ 10 3
                    ♥ 10
                    ♦ K J 10 9 8 7 5 2
                    ♣ Q J

WEST   EAST
♠ Q J 9 8 7 5 4   ♠ A 6 2
♥ 8 3   ♥ K Q J 9 7 6 5
♦ 3   ♦ 4
♣ 7 3 2   ♣ A 8

                    SOUTH
                    ♠ K
                    ♥ A 4 2
                    ♦ A Q 6
                    ♣ K 10 9 6 5 4

The visitors scored a game in both rooms against The Aces —four spades in one room and five diamonds in the other for a total swing of 1,020 points or 14 IMPs.

Peter Pender refused to be intimidated by the preemptive bidding and doubled four spades. His partner, Grant Baze, bid five diamonds and made that contract easily.

THIS QUIZ IS TAKEN FROM A RECENT knockout match played by The Aces in the latter rounds of a national tournament. Match your bids and results with those made at the table.

Question No. 1. You are South, vulnerable, and hold:

♠ K 10 5 4 3 2
♥ —
♦ A 6
♣ A Q 7 6 2

Would you continue on to slam after this bidding?

North	East	South	West
1 ♥	Pass	1 ♠	1 NT
2 ♥	Pass	3 ♣	Pass
5 ♣	Pass	?	

Question No. 2. You are South, vulnerable, and hold:

♠ J 10 7
♥ 5
♦ A Q 9 8 4 2
♣ 7 4 3

What action would you take after:

West	North	East	South
1 ♥	2 ♣	4 ♥	?

Answer No. 1. A pass loses 13 international match points; six clubs gets you a tie. The entire hand:

NORTH
♠ —
♥ A J 10 5 4 2
♦ K 7 3
♣ K 10 5 4

WEST
♠ A Q 8
♥ 9 6
♦ Q J 10 9 8 2
♣ J 8

EAST
♠ J 9 7 6
♥ K Q 8 7 3
♦ 5 4
♣ 9 3

SOUTH
♠ K 10 5 4 3 2
♥ —
♦ A 6
♣ A Q 7 6 2

Ace Bob Hamman continued on to slam to earn a tie. At the other table the opponents had no trouble reaching slam after Ace Jim Jacoby overcalled with a normal two diamonds rather than the frisky one no-trump overcall chosen at Hamman's table.

Answer No. 2. Pass loses 2 IMPs. Double breaks even. Five clubs gains 11 IMPs. Five diamonds will probably lose 5 or 7 IMPs. The entire hand:

NORTH
♠ A 3 2
♥ 4 3
♦ J 6
♣ A K J 10 6 5

WEST
♠ K Q
♥ A Q J 10 8
♦ 10 7 5 3
♣ Q 9

EAST
♠ 9 8 6 5 4
♥ K 9 7 6 2
♦ K
♣ 8 2

SOUTH
♠ J 10 7
♥ 5
♦ A Q 9 8 4 2
♣ 7 4 3

With Aces Mike Lawrence and Bob Hamman holding the East-West cards, South chose to bid a fearless five clubs, which, on the lie of the cards, could not be defeated. At the other table, Ace Bobby Wolff (North) elected to double four hearts in a competitive auction. This was defeated one trick for a net loss of 500 points by The Aces or 11 IMPs.

BOTH OF THESE QUIZ HANDS WERE PLAYED in the early rounds of the Vanderbilt National Knockout Team Championship in Atlanta in March. Place yourself in the decision seat and match your bids with the contestants.

Question No. 1. You are South, no vulnerability, and hold:

♠ 9 8 6 5
♥ 9 7
♦ 9 7 6 4 2
♣ 6 4

What do you bid at this point?

West	North	East	South
1 ♥	Dbl.	4 ♥	Pass
Pass	Dbl.	Pass	?

Question No. 2. Your are South, East-West vulnerable, and hold:

♠ J 10 8 6 3 2
♥ K Q J
♦ 9 8
♣ 5 4

What do you lead against three no-trump after this bidding? (West's double is negative, showing about 6-10 points.)

South	West	North	East
Pass	Pass	Pass	1 ♣
1 ♠	Dbl.	Pass	2 ♣
Pass	2 ♥	Pass	3 NT
Pass	Pass	Pass	

Answer No. 1. Pass loses 170 points, since the opponents can make four hearts doubled. If you bid four spades, you pick up 320 points, going down two undoubled. The entire hand was:

                    NORTH
                    ♠ A Q 10 4 3
                    ♥ J 4
                    ♦ A 8
                    ♣ A K 9 8
WEST   EAST
♠ K 7 2   ♠ J
♥ A K 10 3 2   ♥ Q 8 6 5
♦ J 10 5 3   ♦ K Q
♣ J   ♣ Q 10 7 5 3 2
                    SOUTH
                    ♠ 9 8 6 5
                    ♥ 9 7
                    ♦ 9 7 6 4 2
                    ♣ 6 4

In the match, the Robert Lipsitz team played a four-heart contract in one room and made it against Aces Bob Goldman and Mike Lawrence.

At the other table, against Aces Jim Jacoby and Bobby Wolff, S. H. Labins of West Hartford and Chuck Lamprey of White Plains, N.Y., saved at four spades on the bidding shown above.

The Lipsitz team gained 320 points or 8 international match points in a close match against The Aces.

Answer No. 2. If you led a spade, the opponents ran off nine quick tricks and scored 600 points. A heart lead beats the contract one trick and gives 100 points to your side. The entire hand was:

                    NORTH
                    ♠ 9 7 4
                    ♥ A 8 6 3
                    ♦ A 6 2
                    ♣ 10 9 6
WEST   EAST
♠ K   ♠ A Q 5
♥ 10 9 7 5 4   ♥ 2
♦ Q J 10 4 3   ♦ K 7 5
♣ 3 2   ♣ A K Q J 8 7
                    SOUTH
                    ♠ J 10 8 6 3 2
                    ♥ K Q J
                    ♦ 9 8
                    ♣ 5 4

At one table, Ace Bob Hamman found the killing lead of the heart king to pick up 100 points. At the other table, Aces Jim Jacoby and Bobby Wolff bid the hand as shown above.

Jacoby's negative double, followed by his heart bid, steered South from the winning heart lead and gained The Aces a total of 700 points or 12 IMPs.

THIS QUIZ IS TAKEN FROM THE FINAL session of the 1971 world championship match between France and The Aces.

When these two hands came along, France was fighting gallantly and had reduced a deficit of 45 IMPs to only 30 IMPs, with seven hands to play. Place yourself in the decision chair and bid two critical deals of the world championship.

Question No. 1. You are South, both vulnerable, and hold:

♠ Q
♥ A Q 6 5 4
♦ Q 7 6 5 3
♣ 10 3

What do you do after West's weak bid is passed to you?

East	South	West	North
Pass	Pass	2 ♦	Pass
Pass	?		

Answer No. 1. If you passed, you made the winning decision. West will struggle for six tricks and end up going down. If you bid two hearts, you end up in trouble, since North holds most of the outstanding high cards. The entire hand:

NORTH
♠ K 9 6 2
♥ 8 2
♦ A 9
♣ A K 9 8 6

WEST
♠ J 10 5 4
♥ J
♦ K J 10 8 4 2
♣ 7 5

EAST
♠ A 8 7 3
♥ K 10 9 7 3
♦ —
♣ Q J 4 2

SOUTH
♠ Q
♥ A Q 6 5 4
♦ Q 7 6 5 3
♣ 10 3

At the table, South (Henri Svarc) decided to bid two hearts over Ace Bobby Goldman's two-diamond bid. North (Jean-Michel Boulenger) decided to come to life with a three diamond cue bid and South leaped to a heart game. Ace Mike Lawrence (East) gulped and said "double."

Svarc could not handle the hand and went down three tricks for 800 points (14 IMPs) to The Aces.

Aces Jim Jacoby and Bobby Wolff defeated an East-West contract of two spades in the other room.

Question No. 2. You are South, neither side vulnerable, and hold:

♠ 6 2
♥ 10 9 8 4
♦ K 3
♣ A K J 10 3

What action do you take at this point?

West	North	East	South
1 ♠	2 ♥	4 ♥	?

Answer No. 2. Double loses 590 points, since the opponents will make four spades. Five hearts is the winning bid, as it goes down only one trick. The entire hand:

NORTH
♠ 10
♥ A K J 7 5 3
♦ J 8 6
♣ 9 6 2

WEST
♠ A K Q J 9
♥ Q
♦ 10 7 4
♣ Q 8 7 5

EAST
♠ 8 7 5 4 3
♥ 6 2
♦ A Q 9 5 2
♣ 4

SOUTH
♠ 6 2
♥ 10 9 8 4
♦ K 3
♣ A K J 10 3

At the table, Ace Mike Lawrence made the winning decision to bid five hearts. To add icing to the cake, the opponents continued to five spades, which he doubled and beat one trick.

In the other room, Ace Bobby Wolff played a doubled four-spade contract and made it for a total gain of 690 points or 12 additional IMPs.

These two results increased The Aces' lead to 56 IMPs with only five hands to play and provided a much-needed opportunity for The Aces' rooters to relax.

THE ACES SHARE THE OPINION THAT THE AVER-age bridge player worries too much about point count and not enough about distribution. Take yourself, for example. Do you try to picture your partner's distribution during the bidding?

This little quiz will start you on the right path. Instead of picturing your partner's entire distribution, you must decide only upon the number of spades South is showing in the following eight bidding situations. Get six or more right and your bridge thinking is headed in the right direction.

HOW MANY SPADES?

1. South	North	5. South	North
1 ♣	1 ♠	1 ♠	2 ♣
2 ♠	2 NT	3 ♠	3 NT
3 NT		Pass	
2. South	North	6. South	North
1 ♣	1 ♠	Pass	1 ♠
3 ♠	4 ♠	2 ♦	2 NT
Pass		3 ♠	4 ♠
		Pass	
3. South	North	7. South	North
1 ♥	1 ♠	1 ♦	1 ♠
2 ♦	2 NT	3 ♦	3 ♥
3 ♠	3 NT	4 ♠	Pass
Pass			
4. South	North	8. South	North
1 ♣	1 ♥	1 ♦	1 ♠
1 ♠	1 NT	2 ♦	3 ♣
2 ♠	3 ♣	4 ♣	4 ♠
Pass		Pass	

SOLUTIONS

1. **Three.** With four spades, South would reraise the spades over the two no-trump rebid. With a minimum hand and four spades, he would rebid three spades, and with a maximum

194

hand, he would say four spades. South is showing three spades and a count of 14 or 15 high card points. With less he would simply pass two no-trump, a bid that shows 10-12 high-card points.

2. **Four.** A jump raise promises four-card support.

3. **Three.** Delayed support shows three cards. South's distribution should be five hearts, four diamonds, three spades and one club.

4. **Five.** South is describing a hand with five or six clubs and five spades. Once South rebids spades he promises a five-card suit.

But he opened one club; therefore, his clubs must be as long as or longer than his spades or else he would have opened one spade. (Hands with five clubs and five spades generally should be opened with one club.)

5. **Six.** A jump rebid promises at least a six-card suit.

6. **Three.** Delayed support shows three cards. With four spades, South would have raised immediately.

After an original pass, he could not have risked being left in two diamonds with concealed four-card spade support. (A new suit by responder is not forcing if responder is a passed hand.)

7. **Three.** With four spades, South would have raised spades immediately.

8. **One or two.** South must have six diamonds and four clubs. With five diamonds he would have rebid two clubs over one spade. (South must have four clubs to raise North's *second* suit immediately.) South has either a small doubleton in spades, or hopefully a singleton honor.

Dear Mr. Corn:

In our regular monthly three-table game we managed to flub this hand all three times it was played. The contracts were:

6 NT	down	3
6 ♣	down	3
4 ♦	making	7

How should the hand have been bid?

All vulnerable
Dealer West

                        NORTH
                        ♠ 10 9 7
                        ♥ 9 8
                        ♦ A K J 10 9 7 6
                        ♣ 3

WEST   **EAST**
♠ Q J 8 5   ♠ 4 3 2
♥ Q 10 7 3 2   ♥ K J 5
♦ Q 8 4   ♦ 5 3 2
♣ Q   ♣ 10 8 6 5

                        SOUTH
                        ♠ A K 6
                        ♥ A 6 4
                        ♦ —
                        ♣ A K J 9 7 4 2

                                        Flubbers, Baltimore.

Answer: Your hand is one that might well cause many experienced pairs some grief. I suggest the following after three passes:

South	North
2 ♣	3 ♦
4 ♣	4 ♦
6 ♦	Pass

The jump to slam with a void may appear risky. However, North's bidding promises a good long suit with, at most, one loser. Since North's diamonds can be useful only in a diamond contract, South should give up on playing the hand.

Dear Mr. Corn:

We missed an easy slam after a preemptive bid by our opponents. How should we have bid?

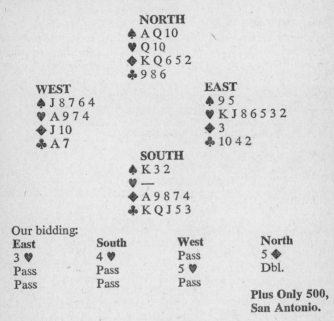

NORTH
- ♠ A Q 10
- ♥ Q 10
- ♦ K Q 6 5 2
- ♣ 9 8 6

WEST
- ♠ J 8 7 6 4
- ♥ A 9 7 4
- ♦ J 10
- ♣ A 7

EAST
- ♠ 9 5
- ♥ K J 8 6 5 3 2
- ♦ 3
- ♣ 10 4 2

SOUTH
- ♠ K 3 2
- ♥ —
- ♦ A 9 8 7 4
- ♣ K Q J 5 3

Our bidding:

East	South	West	North
3 ♥	4 ♥	Pass	5 ♦
Pass	Pass	5 ♥	Dbl.
Pass	Pass	Pass	

Plus Only 500,
San Antonio.

Answer: South had a difficult decision. However, the four-heart cue bid was an overbid that should have easily propelled North to six diamonds. I suggest:

East	South	West	North
3 ♥	Dbl.	4 ♥ (?)	5 ♦
Pass	6 ♦	All pass	

Dear Mr. Corn:

I have two questions. Can you double your partner? Can you re-redouble?

Action Lover,
Baltimore.

Answer: Among other reasons, it would not be sporting to allow a player to double every time his side can make a contract. I can cite no argument against the re-redouble except that one might need a computer to keep score.

I have a sneaking suspicion that a bridge game with you might prove exciting.

Dear Mr. Corn:

Is there a rule, law or regulation that requires the trump suit *always* be spread on dummy's right side? We can't agree and we don't know how to find out.

Equally Divided,
Long Beach, Calif.

Answer: Your question intrigued me so that I searched the International Code on Bridge. Much to my surprise, I found there was a rule rather than a custom. I quote, ". . . dummy spreads his hand . . . with the trumps on his right . . ."

Dear Mr. Corn:

When a revoke has become established, is the two-trick penalty scored above or below the line? I played a hand at two spades and the opponents revoked. I made two, plus the penalty, which totaled four. I claimed a game, but my opponents objected. We are still arguing.

Cheap Game,
Cape Cod, Mass.

Answer: Sorry, but you are not entitled to a game. When your side acquires two tricks as a result of a revoke, they are treated exactly as if they had been won in the normal course of play. Only the trick score contracted for is entered below the line.

Dear Mr. Corn:

The battle is raging. Please send some ammunition. My partner opened one no-trump and we play Jacoby and Texas transfers. My right-hand opponent doubled and I bid two diamonds holding:

♠ 6
♥ Q 9 7 6 4 3
♦ K 6 2
♣ 8 5 4

Would you believe I played it there? To make matters worse, two "local authorities" agree with my partner. Am I wrong? If so, why?

Answer: Sorry but my ammunition will not fit your guns.

While a few players continue the use of conventions after a double, most do not. The reason is primarily one of simplicity to avoid confusion.

Much of the time an interfering overcall eliminates a transfer suit and can cause confusion. Over an opponent's double, the main objective becomes safety and the ability to rescue in clubs or any other suit should get priority.

To eliminate misunderstandings, many players simply agree, "All special conventions are off if the opponents interfere."

Dear Mr. Corn:

This hand really caused some excitement in our bridge game.

```
                    NORTH
                 ♠ K 10 2
                 ♥ 3
                 ♦ A K Q J 10 8 6 4 2
                 ♣ —
WEST                              EAST
♠ A                              ♠ 7 4 3
♥ A K J 8 7 5 2                  ♥ Q 10 9 6
♦ —                              ♦ 9 7 5 3
♣ A 10 6 5 3                     ♣ J 7
                    SOUTH
                 ♠ Q J 9 8 6 5
                 ♥ 4
                 ♦ —
                 ♣ K Q 9 8 4 2
```

Our bidding:

South	West	North	East
1 ♠	2 ♠	6 ♦	Pass
Pass	6 ♥	6 ♠	Pass
Pass	Dbl.		

West led the club ace and the hand was made. How should it have been bid?

Excitement Galore,
Piedmont, Calif.

Answer: Although South's opening bid was rather light, the auction was pinpoint accurate. East-West bid to their maximum contract of six hearts, and North-South bid to their par of six spades (sacrifice). How can I improve on such results?

West's choice of opening lead was a poor one, however, and he paid an extreme penalty for his indiscretion.

There is a lesson here. Since West has control in all suits, he should try to cash a high heart first. If that is ruffed, he can win the very next trick to do whatever may be necessary.

Dear Mr. Corn:

I've heard the phrase "Trump Peter." What does it mean?
Uninformed, Miami

Answer: The peter is a term used in Great Britain, but rarely elsewhere, to describe a high-low in discarding. Many players play high-low in the trump suit to signal partner of a holding of at least three trumps. Most of these players include the additional stipulation that the trump peter shows an ability to ruff something.

Dear Dr. Corn:

Please clarify a treatment I've seen others use. After a takeout double of an opening bid of one, two or three of a suit, responder bids the cheapest possible suit to show a dead hand.

What is the name of this convention?
Bad Cards, Ft.Worth

Answer: The convention you refer to is known as the "Herbert." The convention has few users and for good reason. All too frequently you hold a hand with which you want to bid the suit rather than show the hand strength. For example:

West	North	East	South
1 ♦	Dbl.	Pass	?

Holding:

♠ 5
♥ 10 9 4 2
♦ J 6 4 3 2
♣ Q 7 6

If your bid of one heart shows strength instead of your best

200

suit (opponent's suit excluded), partner will probably bid spades. You are then faced with the unhappy choice of passing with a singleton or bidding on, with the danger of getting too high.

Dear Mr. Corn:

I lost a duplicate game because my partner passed my Blackwood four no-trump bid. These were the hands and the bidding:

NORTH
♠ 9 8 3
♥ J 7 4 3
♦ A 4
♣ K 8 7 3

SOUTH
♠ A K Q J 10
♥ A
♦ K Q 8 7 5 3
♣ 9

South	West	North	East
1 ♦	2 ♣	Dbl.	Pass
3 ♠	Pass	4 ♠	Pass
4 NT	Pass	Pass! !	Pass

The club queen was led, and only my club 9 kept me from going down. My partner said he thought that I had only four spades and that I should have opened with a spade. I think he's nuts. What's your opinion?

> **Left at the Altar,**
> **Palo Alto, Calif.**

Answer: There is no question that North should have responded to your Blackwood bid. He probably was embarrassed about his pass and, like most any other ego-conscious bridge player, transferred the discussion to the number of spades shown by your bidding.

Forgive him if you can. Otherwise loosen your requirements for opening-game demand bids.

Dear Mr. Corn:

I belong to a Senior Citizens' Club and we play three days a week. I can't get an answer to my question in my group and two reference books disagree. I'm sure you can give me the right answer.

When playing Gerber, how does one ask for kings? One book says five clubs; the other says the next ranking suit.

Need Kings,
Lakewood, Calif.

Answer: As written, the Gerber Convention provides for king-asking by bidding the next ranking suit (excepting the agreed trump suit, which is a signoff).

In practice, the problems encountered concerning what was and what wasn't an agreed trump suit resulted in modifications to the convention by various partnerships. They decided to use five clubs as a king-asking bid to avoid misunderstandings. You may play it either way, depending upon your agreement with your partner.

Dear Mr. Corn:

I am bugged by a couple of bridge players who exchange hands after they buy the contract and enter into a prolonged discussion before playing the hand. What is your opinion? Is there any remedy?

Irked, St. Louis

Answer: I don't blame you. Not only are these players very inconsiderate, they are violating the proprieties of the game.

As far as a remedy is concerned, it depends upon your group. The players are definitely out of line and in violation of the written proprieties (Laws of Contract Bridge). Use the direct or indirect approach based on your judgment.

I would recommend tactful handling of the situation if, for example, one of the violators is your husband's boss.

Dear Mr. Corn:

Please help settle a dispute which has caused trouble in my home for over two weeks. My husband and I were defending three no-trump. I led the club 3, my husband won with the ace and returned the 7.

When declarer played the queen, I thought he also had the jack because my partner should have returned the jack had he held it.

My husband says that if he held only three of my suit, he would return his highest remaining card, but if he started with four or more, he should return what was his original fourth best.

This was the club suit:

$$962$$

K 10 4 3   A J 8 7

$$Q 5$$

When declarer played the queen, I let it win so that later partner could lead another club while I still had the king.

Troubles,
Niagara Falls, N.Y.

Answer: While I never like to disagree with a lady, and at the risk of causing more trouble, I will have to side rather strongly with your husband. It is standard practice to play as your husband described.

Incidentally, if you thought your partner's 7 was his highest, then there was no reason to duck the queen. All the clubs smaller than the 7 are in sight and your husband couldn't return another club later if he wanted to. Tell him you're sorry and try to arrange a game of mixed partners.

Dear Mr. Corn:

How do you show aces when the opponents interfere over Blackwood?

As South I had:

♠ A Q 10 8 6 4
♥ 7
♦ A K Q 9 7
♣ 5

The bidding:

North	East	South	West
		1 ♠	2 ♥
3 ♠	4 ♥	4 NT	5 ♥
Pass	Pass	?	

What should I have done?
Partner had:

♠ K J 7 3
♥ 4
♦ J 8 6 4
♣ A Q 3 2

Mr. Milquetoast,
Rochester, N.Y.

Answer: This problem can be aggravating. When you want to know about partner's aces, the last people you want to hear from are the opponents. Especially if, as most other people, you and your partner have not agreed on a method.

I suggest the following simple convention:

Double—no aces; pass—one ace; first step over the interference—two aces, etc.

This works well because when you lack sufficient aces, you can double the opponents and hopefully keep them from being so annoying in the future. This treatment may be easy to remember as DOPI. D (Double)=0; P (Pass)=1.

If North had been using this treatment on the given hand, his pass would have shown one ace and you could have bid the slam.

Dear Mr. Corn:

My partner and I would appreciate the correct auction on the following hands. West deals, both vulnerable.

Hand No. 1:

WEST	EAST
♠ K J 10 9 7 6 4 2	♠ Q
♥ 8	♥ A K Q 10 6 4
♦ A J 10	♦ K Q 4
♣ 9	♣ A J 8

Hand No. 2:

WEST	EAST
♠ A Q 10 9 7	♠ 6
♥ —	♥ Q 10 9 8 7 6 4
♦ A Q	♦ K 9 3
♣ A K 10 8 6 3	♣ 7 2

Hopeless Contract,
Macon, Ga.

Answer: Hand No. 1:

West	East
4 ♠	4 NT
5 ♦	6 ♠

The vulnerable four-spade bid shows less than an opening bid in high cards and the ability to take eight tricks opposite a worthless dummy. East's spade queen is adequate trump support, and when East finds that his side is not missing two aces, a slam is bid. Note that East doesn't consider introducing the heart suit.

Answer: Hand No. 2: Even though West would like to be declarer, he should quit after this auction.

West	East
1 ♣	1 ♥
2 ♠	3 ♥
3 ♠	4 ♥

West has shown five spades and at least five clubs and a very good hand. He should respect East's desire to play in hearts, and there is no reason to repeat what has already been said.

Dear Mr. Corn:

My partner and I had a serious misunderstanding in the bidding of this hand. Would you comment?

WEST	EAST
♠ 9	♠ A K Q J 10 2
♥ K Q 8 7	♥ A 4 3
♦ A Q J 4	♦ K 6 2
♣ K Q 4 3	♣ J

West	East
1 NT	4 NT
Pass	

Misunderstood,
Riverside, Calif.

Answer: It appears there were a number of misunderstandings here. West's one no-trump isn't exactly classic. My guess is that West is East's husband.

East apparently intended four no-trump as Blackwood, asking for aces. East had the right idea but used the wrong approach. Over a one no-trump bid by partner, the four no-trump bid does not ask for aces but says, "I have 15 or 16 points. Do you have a maximum one no-trump opening?" The opener either passes or bids, depending on whether his no-trump bid was minimum or maximum.

Here East should use the four-club convention (Gerber) after the one no-trump bid. This asks for aces and will make it easy for East to bid no-trump.

I prefer this auction.

West	East
1 ♦	2 ♠
3 ♣	4 NT
5 ♦	6 ♠

Dear Mr. Corn:

In a recent duplicate game, I heard someone discussing the "Landy" convention. What is this?

Wondering,
Ft. Wayne, Ind.

Answer: The Landy convention is a device for competing against an opening bid of one no-trump. Over an opponent's one no-trump, a two-club overcall promises nothing about clubs but rather shows length in both major suits. It asks partner to bid his best major.

Usually the Landy bidder has ten cards in hearts and spades. Something like:

> ♠ K Q 10 7 6
> ♥ A J 9 4 2
> ♦ Q 7
> ♣ 6

When using the Landy convention, the double of a one no-trump conveys a desire to defend that contract. It is not a take-out double, since the Landy convention substitutes for the takeout double.

Dear Mr. Corn:

When you open with one no-trump and your partner bids two clubs, asking for a major suit, what do you bid when you have four spades and four hearts?

Trouble Choosing,
Macon, Ga.

Answer: There are several ways to show both major suits. Some players bid two no-trump and some bid three clubs. However, these bids are cumbersome and, in addition to making the bidding difficult for your side, they tell the opponents too much about your hand.

The method I prefer is the simple one of bidding a major suit and later, if necessary, the other. It is a matter of partnership style, whether you bid hearts first or spades first.

Just be sure both partners agree on the procedure being

206

used. If there is no prior partnership agreement, the practice is to bid spades first.

Dear Mr. Corn:

I had a nightmare of an afternoon in a recent social bridge game. Among other disasters, we played this grand slam in game. How would The Aces have bid it?

NORTH	SOUTH
♠ A 6 5	♠ K Q J 9 8 7
♥ 7	♥ A K 9 8 4 3 2
♦ J 10 7 2	♦ —
♣ A J 10 9 2	♣ —

Our bidding:

East	South	West	North
1 ♦	2 ♦	Pass	3 ♣
Pass	3 ♥	Pass	3 NT
Pass	4 ♥	Pass	Pass
Pass			

Missed It, Detroit

Answer: It must have been quite an afternoon to cause South to overlook that six-card spade suit! I gave the hand to Aces Bob Goldman and Mike Lawrence and they bid:

East	South	West	North
1 ♦	2 ♦	Pass	3 ♣
Pass	3 ♥	Pass	3 NT
Pass	4 ♠	Pass	5 ♠
Pass	5 NT*	Pass	6 ♦**
Pass	7 ♠		

*How many trump honors have you?
**I have one (responses same as Blackwood responses).

Dear Mr. Corn:

My partner feels that I should have bid six diamonds and I feel he should have. Who's right?

WEST	EAST
♠ A 6 5 2	♠ K 5
♥ K Q 7	♥ 6 3
♦ —	♦ A Q J 10 7 5 4 3
♣ A K Q 10 7 3	♣ 9

West	East
1 ♣	2 ♦
4 ♣	4 ♦
4 ♠	5 ♦
5 ♥	6 ♣
Pass	

As it turns out, six diamonds would have made, but I went down in six clubs.

Wrong Minor, Detroit

Answer: I am afraid that you've asked me the wrong question. Six diamonds is a very poor slam and one you surely wouldn't want to reach. Your question should have been, "How do we stop at five diamonds?"

I suggest the following auction:

West	East
1 ♣	1 ♦
2 ♠	3 ♦
3 NT	5 ♦
Pass	

Dear Mr. Corn:

My partner opened with three spades and I bid four hearts holding:

♠ 9 2
♥ A K J 9 7 6
♦ A 3
♣ K J 7

My left-hand opponent doubled and I went down two. My partner was angry with me. Was I wrong?

Good Suits, San Antonio

Answer: Yes. Twice. You should have raised your partner to four spades instead of bidding four hearts. You knew the partnership had a good spade fit, but you were gambling on hearts.

Your left-hand opponent erred when he gave you another chance by doubling. Since you missed the chance to correct, you owe your partner two apologies.

Dear Mr. Corn:

What is the proper response to a Blackwood four no-trump

when holding two aces and a void? Responder has not had an opportunity to cue-bid his void suit.

Need A Method,
Baltimore

Answer: There are several ways to solve the problem. One of the easiest to remember, and the one I prefer is:

Bid—Four no-trump. Response—Five no-trump (shows two aces and a void).

Bid—Four no-trump. Response—Six of a suit lower than the agreed trump suit (one ace and a void in the bid suit).

Bid—Four no-trump. Response—Six of the trump suit (one ace and a void in a higher ranking suit).

If you hold no aces and a void, bid five clubs and then decide later if you wish to go on.

In adopting conventions or methods to cover rare situations, memory is an important consideration. Therefore, I suggest that the easier the method is to remember, the better.

Dear Mr. Corn:

We missed a grand slam on the following hand. How should it be bid?

WEST	EAST
♠ K Q J 10 9 3	♠ A 8 7 2
♥ A	♥ K J 5 4
♦ A 2	♦ J 6 4 3
♣ A K 10 5	♣ Q

Our bidding:

West	East
2 ♠	4 ♠
4 NT	5 ♦
6 ♠	Pass

Missed It,
New Cumberland, Pa.

Answer: East should not have jumped to four spades over two spades. There is no reason to reduce your bidding space when holding a good hand opposite a game demand. I suggest:

West	East	
2 ♠	3 ♠	(Positive response)
4 ♣	4 ♥	(Strength showing)
4 NT	5 ♦	(One ace)
5 NT	6 ♦	(One king)
7 ♠		

The three-spade bid promises a positive response and makes it possible to exchange valuable information. The grand-slam bid depends on finding a favorable club holding in dummy. (Note that any singleton or doubleton would suffice.)

Dear Mr. Corn:

After this bidding, East and South jumped on West for passing. The contract was made with overtricks. I think they are wrong. How about you?

North	East	South	West
1 ♥	Dbl.	Rdbl.	Pass
Pass	Pass		

Public Defender,
Palm Springs, Calif.

Answer: I agree with you. West is not obligated to bid after South's redouble unless they have agreed to play "Pass redoubles for penalties." Obviously there was no such agreement and East should take the blame.

Dear Mr. Corn:

In a recent duplicate game I missed a slam on the following bidding. This was my hand (East) and the bidding:

> ♠ A 3
> ♥ K
> ♦ K 9 6 5 4 2
> ♣ J 5 4 3

East	South	West	North
Pass	Pass	4 ♠	Pass
Pass	Pass		

Can you comment on the bidding? Partner's hand was:

> ♠ 10 9 8 7 6 5 2
> ♥ A 2
> ♦ A 3
> ♣ A K

Silenced,
Blythe, Calif.

Answer: After West's four-spade opening, East had a clear-cut pass. I think West was gambling too much when he bid four spades. An opening of one spade would have been much safer with little risk of missing a reasonable four-spade contract.

The slam is only a so-so slam and you should not regret missing it. Without an even trump division, there would have been no play.

Dear Mr. Corn:

My partner claims I won't support her. As South I held:

♠ 6
♥ J 8 4
♦ 6 2
♣ A K Q 10 9 7 4

Who's right on the bidding?

South	West	North	East
1 ♣	Pass	1 ♥	1 ♠
2 ♣	Pass	2 ♦	Pass
3 ♣	Pass	3 NT	Pass
All pass			

Trapped Spade,
Baltimore.

Answer: After reading your first sentence I almost referred your letter to our legal department, and I'm afraid that after you read my answer, you'll wish I had!

Your first two bids were acceptable. However, at your third turn, you should have shown partner that you had some hearts. A two-heart bid in this situation merely says you prefer hearts to diamonds, and, in view of this, J-8-4 of hearts is a nice holding.

Dear Mr. Corn:

Kindly explain the psychic bid. How does one recognize when an opponent is making such a bid against him?

Bluffed,
New Orleans.

Answer: A psychic bid takes two common forms. One is to make a bid representing values not possessed; the other is to bid a suit not held. The purpose is to confuse the opponents.

Recognizing such a bid ranges from not so easy to impossible. Usually the psychic bidder, having laid his smoke screen, will pass at his next turn, even when it appears that he should be bidding.

I do not care for psychic bids myself and my suggestion is —don't.

Dear Mr. Corn:

One of our foursome claims that it is permissible for one partner to inform the other that they have a part score and that the current bid is sufficient to complete the game.

I think she is all wet. Can you clarify please?

Waning Patience,
St. Louis.

Answer: The state of the score can be discussed prior to the start of the bidding. Once the bidding starts, and continuing until the hand is completely played, any discussion concerning the state of the score is considered unethical.

Dear Mr. Corn:

Please tell me how to use the Stayman Convention after an interference bid by the opponents.

Assuming that three clubs is the proper method, do I respond with three diamonds if I have no major? Suppose the interference bid was two diamonds?

Looked Everywhere,
Lafayette, Calif.

Anwer: After interference by the opponents, the proper method to inquire about major suits is to make an immediate cue bid. For example:

South	West	North
1 NT	2 ◆	3 ◆

North's three-diamond bid takes the place of a Stayman two-club bid. The opening bidder bids a major suit if he has one. Lacking that, he bids three no-trump.

If North had bid three clubs instead of three diamonds, that bid would be considered a competitive bid and not the Stayman Convention.

Since the cue bid virtually commits the hand to game, responder must have sufficient values to make a game a reasonable venture.

212

Dear Mr. Corn:

In one of your recent columns you reported that a Mr. Stern bid an opening four spades without knowing the lay of the hand. I find this very strange indeed. Please explain his reasons if you know him.

Skeptical, Dallas.

Answer: I do know Mr. Roger Stern, and I think I know why he bid four spades.

Bids made at high levels are known as preemptive bids. The main purpose is to make it difficult for the opponents to bid conveniently.

A four-spade opening says, "I have seven or eight spades and not enough high cards to justify an opening one-spade bid." If vulnerable, the preemptor usually promises that he can win about eight tricks; if not vulnerable, he usually promises about seven tricks.

Dear Mr. Corn:

Please answer two questions for me. Does dummy ask when partner does not follow suit, "No hearts, partner?" What exactly can dummy say?

How does one know whether a four-club bid is asking for aces (Gerber convention) or if it is a club suit, the four-club bidder having bid clubs previously?

Too Many Answers,
Baltimore.

Answer: Dummy may ask declarer "No hearts, partner?" in an attempt to prevent a revoke. Dummy may also draw attention to any irregularity. For example, dummy might warn declarer against leading from the wrong hand. Dummy may not participate in the play, comment on bidding or play, draw attention to the score, etc.

Distinguishing between a four-club bid as a suit or as the Gerber convention after clubs have been bid is much too confusing for even the most-experienced partnerships. I use Blackwood any time clubs have been bid as a suit. Better to lose a little efficiency than add confusion.

Dear Mr. Corn:

Is a one-club opener a demand bid? We four queens argue over this. We like a club opener, don't like a one-diamond response showing "nothing"—preferring a pass with less than six points. However, from there on it's bedlam!

Help,
St. Louis.

Answer: Some systems, mostly based on Italian methods, play that a one-club opener is a demand bid. Most systems played in this country treat the one-club opener as any other one level bid—not forcing.

I agree 100 percent about a pass being best to show a bad hand regardless of what suit partner may open in at the one level.

Dear Mr. Corn:

Please answer a seemingly unsolvable problem. I have done extensive research and have found eight authorities equally divided on this subject.

What is the game score for a fulfilled doubled and redoubled contract? Is the undoubled score doubled or quadrupled?

Dead End,
Kirkwood, Mo.

Answer: I am assuming that by game score, you mean trick score. The trick score for a double contract is doubled; for a redoubled contract, quadrupled. The game bonus, which is probably what has caused the confusion, remains unchanged.

Dear Mr. Corn:

How does a player inform his partner of a void in a suit?

Can Trump,
South Lyon, Mich.

Answer: There are various ways to indicate voids. The subject is complex, and complete understanding and agreement by the partnership is absolutely necessary. Some players use a jump bid which has no natural meaning to indicate a void in the suit. Many players cue-bid an opponent's suit to show the ace, king, singleton or void. While ambiguous, the hope is that future bidding will clarify matters. And, finally, the auction may be planned in such a way to show the void (bidding three suits, one of them known to be at least five cards).

Dear Mr. Corn:

Never has our group become so heated and upset. Please settle the issue.

We play opening two bids forcing to game. However, one of our players decided to stop short of game after having opened with a demand bid (the opponents intervened and he devalued his hand). Is this a violation of the rules and is it any concern of the opponents? Can they force him to bid again or do they have any voice in the matter?

White Hot,
Searcy, Ark.

Answer: A player is entitled to make any bid he desires, consistent with the laws and proprieties of contract bridge. Although a player may have agreed to play a specific system, there is no law which prohibits him from deviating from his announced system, provided there is no private understanding. Such deviations, however, are not likely to promote partnership harmony and efficiency.

As far as the opponents are concerned, they have no rights concerning your "bridge" decisions. You'll hear enough from partner without having to hear from them! Thus, if you are convinced it is proper to pass an 18-point hand with no long suits, while a bad practice, it is just not an opponent's business.

P.S. Have you ever heard the opponents demand a player bid a game he could have made?

Dear Mr. Corn:

Can a player announce to his partner and opponents that he is going to make a jump bid? I have played many years without knowing this but was recently informed by a player who came from another state.

Quiet Jumps,
Fort Worth.

Answer: The American Contract Bridge League adopted the "skip-bid warning" rule for duplicate bridge. Its intent is to reduce the element of surprise of preemptive bids—such surprise increasing the possibility of conveying illegal information (i.e., a slow pass vs. a quick one). The rule makes it mandatory for the next player to wait at least ten seconds before making any bid after a skip-bid announcement. This rule does not apply to rubber or party bridge, unless, of course, all parties agree to adopt the procedure.

Dear Mr. Corn:

What is the right play at trick one? We were in seven hearts and West led the heart 6.

NORTH
♠ A K 10 8 7
♥ A 5 4 2
♦ A K J
♣ A

SOUTH
♠ 6
♥ Q J 10 9 7 3
♦ 8
♣ K Q 10 5 4

The bidding:

North	South
2 ♠	3 ♥
4 ♥	4 NT
5 ♣	5 NT
6 ♥	7 ♥

Lost A Grand, Chicago.

Answer: I assume the five-club bid showed zero or all four aces, and this information was also known by West. Normally, I would play the ace. But this situation, where dummy is known to hold four aces, greatly increases the chances that West is making a sneaky lead from K-6 of trumps.

My play would have to be influenced by my knowledge of the person on lead. Is he an average player, a clever player, imaginative, etc.? Was the lead made casually or was it made deliberately after prolonged thought?

Unless the above considerations were to sway my feelings, I would play the ace at the first trick.

Dear Mr. Corn:

In a recent duplicate, my partner opened one no-trump (16-18) and my right-hand opponent doubled. I held:

♠ Q 10 7
♥ K 10 9 7
♦ K 7 6 5
♣ 4 2

Then I redoubled. My partner thought it was an SOS and removed to two clubs. I passed, thinking my partner might be psyching. We made three, but it was a poor result.

Suspicious, Boston.

Answer: It is good practice to use the redouble to indicate some high cards and a willingness to double the opponents. If your right-hand opponent bids after your redouble, you would double two spades, hearts or diamonds, and would pass two clubs to your partner, the message being, "I can't double this, but I have a few points. What do you think?"

Incidentally, the idea that you thought partner was psyching worked against you. This practice is a loser in the long run. Here you could have bid two no-trump after partner's two clubs and gotten back on the right track except for the worry that partner had nothing but clubs.

Dear Mr. Corn:

The opponents bid one no-trump—three no-trump. I led the heart 10, hoping to set up partner's suit. I was told this was very wrong. However, my partner's reasons seemed to be based upon results rather than logic. Please give me the straight dope.

♠ J 10 7
♥ 10
♦ 8 6 4 2
♣ 9 7 6 5 3

Wrong Again?, Shreveport.

Answer: With this hopeless hand, you were probably right not to lead a club. Since the opponents did not look for a major suit fit, it was reasonable to assume that partner had length in either spades, or hearts, or both.

The argument against leading a heart is simple. If you find partner with five of them, it means the opponents have seven. It is likely that declarer will attack hearts himself, and your heart lead may easily help him play the suit to his best advantage.

Only if partner has six hearts is the lead likely to help him, and even then, only occasionally. My choice would be the spade jack.

Dear Mr. Corn:

Please comment on our bidding of this hand. We defended well against two spades, taking two clubs and a club ruff, two hearts, a diamond and two spade tricks for eight tricks and a 500-point penalty. As you can see, we could have made six diamonds. Where did we go wrong?

217

East-West vulnerable
Dealer South

NORTH
- ♠ 4
- ♥ 10 9 8 6 4
- ♦ 6 5 2
- ♣ 8 7 5 2

WEST
- ♠ J 8 7 5 2
- ♥ K 5
- ♦ Q 7 3
- ♣ A 9 6

EAST
- ♠ Q
- ♥ A J 7 3
- ♦ A K J 9 8 4
- ♣ K 3

SOUTH
- ♠ A K 10 9 6 3
- ♥ Q 2
- ♦ 10
- ♣ Q J 10 4

The bidding:

South	West	North	East
1 ♠	Pass	Pass	Dbl.
2 ♠	Dbl.	All pass	

Short Points,
Scarsdale, N.Y.

Answer: When an opponent opens the bidding, it is difficult to bid a slam with any sense of assurance. This hand is no exception.

The bidding was very reasonable and the only questionable bid was East's final pass. I happen to agree with East's decision. If West's hand were changed slightly, the penalty could have easily been more and no slam on for East-West.

In all, I think you were a bit unlucky.

Dear Mr. Corn:

Please clarify the rules for me concerning this bidding:

North	East	South	West
1 ♦	Pass	2 ♣	2 ♥
2 ♦	Pass		

Overruled,
Bloomsburg, Pa.

I was West and said to North, "You made an insufficient
218

bid." South replied, "That may be so, but East's pass condones the bid and it stands." Is South right?

Answer: South gave you the right dope. An insufficient bid becomes a legal bid if the next player makes a bid before his side calls attention to the irregularity.

Dear Mr. Corn:

If you answer my question, it will be the third lesson I've received concerning this lead problem. I welcome yours but the other two were unsolicited (from my partner and my opponent).

I was on lead against three no-trump after my left-hand opponent used Stayman. I held the K-J-10-5-2 of hearts and led the 5. Was I wrong?

Free Lessons,
Redlands, Calif.

Answer: On the bidding given, there was a good chance that dummy had four hearts. The lead of an honor would have blocked the suit if your partner had as little as 9-x. So your lead was correct.

However, if the bidding had been one no-trump—three no-trump, the lead of the jack would have been correct.

Dear Mr. Corn:

One of my bridge partners believes anything goes in bidding a preemptive bid. The other day she opened with three hearts—it was a new rubber with no score. She had one point in her hand—a jack which wasn't even in her suit! She had seven hearts, 9 high. I had 18 points and bid four hearts. We went down two.

I told her she shouldn't have bid at all. She claims I'm all wet. Who's right?

On A Roller Coaster,
Manchester, Conn.

Answer: Preemptive bids as with everything else about bridge, is a partnership matter and not an individual one. Therefore, an agreement on how your partnership preempts, plus consistent discipline, is more important than whether these bids are weak or strong.

My personal preference is to have a decent suit when I preempt. Naturally, much depends upon vulnerability, since I do not like large penalties any more than anyone else.

Sounds as though your partner is not going to change her ways. If you want to continue to play with her and achieve reasonable results, I suggest you accede to her desires. Even if her treatment is inferior, at least you'll both be aware of the patterns and will have to guess less.

Dear Mr. Corn:

Our partnership needs help. We can't agree and we can't find the answer in any reference book. Can you settle the problem please?

Here's the problem. My partner sat North and I was South.

NORTH
♠ K 8
♥ 10 9 7
♦ Q J 10 5 3
♣ A K 4

SOUTH
♠ A 9 3
♥ A K 6 5 3
♦ 6 4
♣ Q 5 2

The bidding:

North	East	South	West
Pass	Pass	1 ♥	2 ♣
3 ♦	Pass	Pass	Pass

She maintains that the jump bid is forcing. I say that the only forcing bid is a cue bid of three clubs. She had passed with 13 points!

Unforced,
Colorado Springs.

Answer: The Aces play, as is more or less conventional, that a jump shift after passing is a forcing bid. What makes your question interesting, and apparently confusing to the partnership, is that West's two-club overcall makes another forcing bid available—the cue bid.

I play both bids forcing. The jump shift should show a hand with a good fit and a good side suit (example A); the cue bid should show a good fit and general strength (example B). Examples:

A. ♠ A 9 8 2   B. ♠ A 9 8 2
   ♥ 3   ♥ K Q 10 4
   ♦ K Q J 10 4 3   ♦ 10 9 8 7 6
   ♣ 6 2   ♣ —

Dear Mr. Corn:

Please settle a question for me. I have asked others; but every answer I get is different.

What is the proper prodecure when one player is left with only one card to play, while the others still have two?

The last time this came up, our game turned out to be better than a Cassius Clay fight. Our game is never going to be the same until this is settled.

Wednesday Bridge Club,
Seattle.

Answer: Your question is a common one, and many players find it perplexing. The problem is covered by the Laws of Contract Bridge, 1963 (Part III, page 11).

In general, every player is responsible for starting the deal with all thirteen of his cards. If he is careless, then he may be subject to a penalty.

Specifically, when a player is short a card, whether the missing card was accidentally played to an earlier trick, dropped on the floor, or mixed in with the other deck, it is returned to the proper hand.

If the player revoked because of the absence of the missing card, the revoke penalty must be paid. If the player lost one or more tricks because he did not get to use the card to best advantage, he is out of luck.

If the deck was defective, including any case in which due search for the missing card is unsuccessful, there must be a redeal.

I hope your club returns to normal and that my answer will help prevent dispute in the future.

Dear Mr. Corn:

When should honors be declared at rubber bridge?

Big Holder,
Castroville, Texas.

Answer: Honors should be declared at the conclusion of play. Declarer may declare them earlier if he wishes; however, he is under no obligation to do so. A defender should not declare honors until play is concluded, since his partner is not entitled to the information during the play.

The laws do not specify any time limits on claims, and procedure should be in accordance with local agreements.

Dear Mr. Corn:

I lost a recent duplicate game because of my result on this hand.

My partner (South) held:

♠ K J 3
♥ A J 8 7 2
♦ 9 4 3
♣ 4 2

The bidding went:

South	West	North	East
Pass	Pass	1 ♠	Pass
2 ♥	Pass	3 ♣	Pass
?			

What should South have bid?

Need An Opinion,
Elmwood City, Pa.

Answer: Finding the correct bid after an original pass often requires a compromise.

I do not agree with South's response of two hearts. Since South had passed originally and since two hearts was not a forcing bid, I would bid either two or three spades (an overbid) depending upon mood, system and partner.

As the bidding took place, I would lose no time in bidding four spades over three clubs.

Dear Mr. Corn:

Our group is sharply divided on my question. Would you please settle our differences? We play Standard American.

What was my best bid after a one-diamond opening by partner, a one-spade response by me, and a two-diamond rebid by partner?

I held:

♠ A J 7 2
♥ 8 4
♦ J 6 3
♣ K Q J 7

Undecided,
Springfield, Mass.

Answer: First choice is three clubs, second choice is three diamonds. The bid of three clubs enables partner to bid three no-trump with hearts stopped. However, neither bid is perfect. Three clubs may bring about a game you cannot make, while three diamonds is a decided underbid.

Dear Mr. Corn:

My partner's take-out double was redoubled by my right-hand opponent. Am I released from bidding with "no-count" hands?

Too Many Obligations,
Honolulu.

Answer: You are released from your obligation to bid. Some people play a pass in this position as a penalty pass. However, this is a special treatment and is not recommended.

While released from the obligation to bid, doubler's partner should always bid when he can suggest the most suitable place to play the hand.

For example, holding:

♠ 7 2
♥ 9 8 5 4 2
♦ 7 6 5
♣ 8 3 2

best procedure is to bid one heart after a minor suit opening is doubled and redoubled.

Dear Mr. Corn:

Almost every time we have a revoke, there is a substantial difference of opinion of what constitutes a revoke and the penalty due. Please clarify once and for all.

Changing Times,
Baltimore.

Answer: A revoke in any of the first eleven tricks is established when the offender or his partner leads or plays to the following trick. When established, the penalty (after play ceases) is a maximum of two tricks. Tricks lost by a revoke penalty must have been won during or after the revoke trick. If no tricks were won during this period, there is no penalty. If only one trick was won the penalty is one trick. Tricks won before the revoke cannot be forfeited.

A revoke on the twelfth trick never becomes established,

but it must be corrected if discovered before the cards are mixed together. In this case offender's partner can be required by the injured to play to the twelfth trick either of two cards he could legally have played to that trick.

Dear Mr. Corn:

Against a mama-papa 1H-2H-4H, my partner led the ace and then the king of spades. He then led a diamond. I won and led a spade, thinking he could ruff. I was wrong and declarer ruffed instead.

How should my partner have played spades on lead with A-K-Q?

> Wrong Again,
> San Francisco.

Answer: The great majority of players play that the ace followed by the king shows a doubleton. A few of the avant-garde play ace from A-K regardless of number.

Lacking specific agreement, your play was perfectly correct.

Dear Mr. Corn:

How do you count singleton honors?

> Confused,
> Novato, Calif.

Answer: No one is ever sure of the worth of unguarded honors. For simplicity I recommend one point be deducted for any singleton honor lower than the ace.

There are various ways to evaluate doubleton queens, tripleton jacks, etc. The fact is that initial hand evaluation is only a guide to be changed as more information becomes available in the bidding. In general, promote unguarded honors to full value when partner bids the suit. Demote them to little or no value when opponents bid the suit.